MAGNA
CARTA

AND ITS GIFTS TO CANADA

MAGNA CARTA

AND ITS GIFTS TO CANADA

Democracy, Law, and Human Rights

CAROLYN HARRIS

DUNDURN
TORONTO

Editor: Michael Melgaard
Design: Laura Boyle
Printer: Webcom
Cover Design: Sarah Beaudin
Magna Carta photo: "British Library Cotton MS Augustus II.106," public domain. Source: the British Library; Painting/image: British Library/Robana

Library and Archives Canada Cataloguing in Publication

Harris, Carolyn, 1984-, author
Magna Carta and its gifts to Canada : democracy, law, and human rights / author, Carolyn Harris.

Issued in print and electronic formats.
ISBN 978-1-4597-3112-7 (pbk.).--ISBN 978-1-4597-3113-4 (pdf).--ISBN 978-1-4597-3114-1 (epub)

1. Civil rights--Canada. 2. Magna Carta. I. Title.

KE4381.H37 2015   323.0971   C2014-908135-9
                                                         C2014-908136-7

1   2   3   4   5   19   18   17   16   15

We acknowledge the support of the **Canada Council for the Arts** and the **Ontario Arts Council** for our publishing program. We also acknowledge the financial support of the **Government of Canada** through the **Canada Book Fund** and **Livres Canada Books**, and the **Government of Ontario** through the **Ontario Book Publishing Tax Credit** and the **Ontario Media Development Corporation**.

Care has been taken to trace the ownership of copyright material used in this book. The author and the publisher welcome any information enabling them to rectify any references or credits in subsequent editions.
J. Kirk Howard, President

The publisher is not responsible for websites or their content unless they are owned by the publisher.

Printed and bound in Canada.

VISIT US AT
Dundurn.com | @dundurnpress | Facebook.com/dundurnpress | Pinterest.com/Dundurnpress

Dundurn
3 Church Street, Suite 500
Toronto, Ontario, Canada
M5E 1M2

For my parents, Richard and Sue Harris

Magna Carta and other charters of freedom, and Parliament itself, though nurtured in English soil, have matured when their seeds have been planted in the far corners of the earth.

— Prime Minister John Diefenbaker

Contents

Foreword

It has been a great pleasure to lend my support to the tireless work of Len Rodness, Suzy Rodness, and the entire team at Magna Carta Canada. Thanks to their initiative and hard work, Canadians across our country will have a chance to view an original copy of Magna Carta and its companion document, the Charter of the Forest, on Canadian soil in 2015. I encourage all Canadians, and especially young Canadians, to take advantage of this potentially once-in-a-lifetime opportunity to see an original copy of this eight-hundred-year-old document, and to take a moment to learn more about the historical significance of Magna Carta.

When I was a teenager my father gave me a framed replica of Magna Carta as a gift. While I may not initially have fully appreciated the merits of such a gift, it nonetheless hung in my bedroom and eventually became an object of my curiosity.

Growing up, my father and I frequently discussed historical issues and often Magna Carta became a sort of frame of reference for many of our discussions. As I went on to pursue my studies at university in history and political science — and as I took my first job in politics — that framed gift came with me, both as inspiration for my interests and as a foundational reference for my own beliefs.

One of the great strengths of Magna Carta — and indeed one of the reasons for its enduring legacy — is that there is a little bit in there for nearly everyone. When we consider its place in history it is in some ways surprisingly comprehensive. Not only did it break ground in terms of establishing the primacy of the rule of law, but it also spoke to issues like the balance of power in politics, limits on government, individual rights, prohibition against arbitrary arrest, the economy, the independence of the Church, and many others. If you have a general interest in political science, there is certainly a strong likelihood that those specific issues you care most about can trace some reference to a clause contained in Magna Carta.

While the breadth of material contained within Magna Carta is certainly noteworthy, I think that its most fascinating characteristic is that it represented a revolution seeking to uphold the vast majority of a particular order, rather than an effort to bring an entire order down and start anew. Most revolutions or civil wars throughout history have sought either to achieve "regime change" or to turn the economic or social order upside down. At Runnymede, the barons were not trying to install a new ruler, or abolish long standing institutions. They were trying to protect these institutions by boldly putting forth basic and immutable limits on rulers. It signalled a desire to end the arbitrary and punitive use of power that was all too common to absolute rule. In many ways, it was a traditionalist revolution.

Fundamentally, Magna Carta is an acknowledgement of the inherent rights of human beings; rights that are found in natural law, not the positive law of kings or princes. That even the absolute power of a monarch has natural limits. As a result space was created for parliaments, for the notion that governors required the consent of the governed, and eventually for democracy itself.

While the document was annulled not long after receiving King John's seal, the principles enshrined in Magna Carta and the overarching idea that there are natural limits to political power, nevertheless endured. Indeed the very idea of Magna Carta became so popular that King John's successors had little choice but to reissue the document. With time, and with successive monarchs renewing their commitment to the principles of Magna Carta, it became a political institution unto itself. What began as a bold and even revolutionary idea, had taken hold.

The issuance of Magna Carta was, in many ways, the birth of our system of government and why this year's celebrations are so significant.

It has truly been a personal thrill to be involved in the efforts to bring an original copy of Magna Carta to Canada in 2015. Once again I want to thank Len Rodness, Suzy Rodness, and the entire Magna Carta Canada team for their hard work providing a wonderful celebration of the eight-hundredth anniversary of Magna Carta here in Canada.

In closing, I am especially looking forward to sharing this experience with my own children, and perhaps purchasing a framed copy for them, much in the same way my father did for me so many years ago. While it may be that, like me, they will not immediately appreciate such a gift, I can only hope that they too will one day grow to realize that Magna Carta is in fact among the greatest gifts that we have ever passed down from one generation to the next.

I congratulate Magna Carta Canada for their wonderful work and thank them for providing so many Canadians with this truly once in a lifetime opportunity.

Andrew Scheer, MP
Speaker of the House of Commons

Introduction
Magna Carta at Eight Hundred

Eight hundred years after King John affixed his seal to Magna Carta at the insistence of his rebel barons, one of the rare fourteenth-century versions of the Great Charter is coming to Canada. An edition of Magna Carta issued by Edward I, will be touring Canada in 2015 with stops at the Canadian Museum of History in Gatineau, the Fort York National Historic Site in Toronto, the Canadian Museum for Human Rights in Winnipeg, and the Legislative Assembly of Alberta Visitor Centre in Edmonton. This exhibition is not the first time one of the surviving versions of Magna Carta has come to Canada. In 2010, a 1217 Magna Carta was exhibited at the Manitoba Legislative Building. While Magna Carta was in Winnipeg, Queen Elizabeth II visited the city and unveiled a stone from Runnymede Meadow that she selected herself. The stone became the cornerstone of the Canadian Museum for Human Rights.

The global significance of Magna Carta is well known. The Great Charter is the first example of an English king accepting limits on his power imposed by his subjects, and its terms set precedents for a broad range of modern legal rights, including equality before the law, due process, trial by peers, and freedom from forced marriage. These rights informed the Petition of Right and the development of the constitutional monarchy in the United Kingdom, the American and French Revolutions, and the United Nations' Universal Declaration of Human Rights. In the United States, Magna Carta has been quoted since the seventeenth century as a foundation document for individual property rights in addition to legal rights. In books that examine the global impact of Magna Carta, however, Canada is rarely mentioned outside the history of the British Empire.

Magna Carta has had a profound impact on history, politics, and law in Canada. The Great Charter informed the development of common law in English Canada and continues to be cited in Canadian judicial proceedings. The principles codified in Magna Carta shaped the Royal Proclamation of 1763, which provides the framework for the Crown's relationship with Canada's First Nations. At the time of Confederation in 1867, Canada inherited Britain's unwritten constitution, which was informed by Magna Carta and its successor documents, the Petition of Right and the Bill of Rights. These successor documents transformed England into a constitutional monarchy. Canada shares this system of government with fifteen other Commonwealth realms. These implicit principles in Canada's constitutional framework became explicit with the federal Bill of Rights in 1960 and the Canadian Charter of Rights and Freedoms, which forms the first part of the 1982 Constitution Act.

The Magna Carta 2015 Canada touring exhibition highlights the unique impact of the Great Charter on Canada and the rest of the world. Neither King John nor his rebel barons expected Magna Carta to outlast the unique political circumstances of 1215, but the ideals enshrined in Magna Carta outlasted the thirteenth century to influence the making of the modern world.

▸ There are four surviving versions of Magna Carta from 1215. This eight-hundred-year-old document is housed in the British Library.

Part 1
The History of Kings, Barons, and the Commons

On its eight-hundredth anniversary, Magna Carta remains one of the most influential documents in history. It is the earliest example of an English monarch accepting the will of his subjects by allowing them to impose limits on his power. The charter presented to King John in Runnymede Meadow in 1215 would go on to become the foundation document for modern systems of democratic governance.

The supporters of Magna Carta, however, would be surprised by its current interpretation. In thirteenth-century England, democracy was synonymous with chaos, society was organized by a strict hierarchy, and the charter was written to bind the king to past precedents rather than new responsibilities.

EARLY PERCEPTIONS OF DEMOCRACY

The Ancient Greeks practised an early form of direct democracy that inspired modern forms of government. Classical Athenian democracy (from the Greek *dēmokratía* or rule of the people — as opposed to *aristokratia* or rule of the elite) emerged in the fifth century B.C.E. Citizens were given the right to address the government and could be chosen by lot to form a ruling council. The definition of citizenship, however, was limited. According to the citizenship law, only sons of an Athenian father and mother were eligible to become citizens themselves. Women, slaves, former slaves, foreigners, and men under the age of twenty were all excluded from the political process.

Despite the exclusivity of Athenian citizenship, prominent Greek philosophers argued that democracy was little better than rule by the mob. Plato, author of *The Republic,* theorized that the ideal form of government was rule by philosopher kings who loved knowledge

◄ *The School of Athens* by Raphael (1483–1520). The Athenian philosophers Plato (in purple and red) and Aristotle (in blue and brown) are depicted at the centre of the fresco.

Roman citizens were divided into two classes, one that had the right to marry and accumulate property, and one that could vote and run for political office in addition to these basic rights. As Rome expanded its borders, the two-tiered citizenship structure allowed the elites of new regions to join the Roman political structure gradually without threatening existing interests. The Romans arrived in the British Isles in 43 B.C.E. and ruled much of modern-day England and Wales until 409 C.E., bringing their political traditions with them.

After the collapse of the Western Roman Empire in the fifth century, Germanic tribes from mainland Europe, including the Angles, Saxons, and Jutes, invaded England.

for its own sake. In contrast, he saw democracy as a kind of anarchy where a vast lower class made decisions governed by their baser instincts, most notably the desire for wealth, breaking laws to achieve these goals. Plato's student, Aristotle, judged democracy to be more moderate but still undesirable because it allowed the poor to rule in the interests of their social station without regard for the wider polity. Classical Athens, the society that invented a form of democracy, had strong doubts about the desirability of this system of government.

The Roman Republic (509–27 B.C.E.) drew upon Athenian political ideals but limited democracy to an even narrower group of people. It was a system designed to maintain the power of landowners over labourers. Membership in the Senate, the advisory body of the republic, was limited by age and property qualifications.

◥ *Plato and Aristotle in Discussion* by Luca della Robbia, 1437. These two Athenian philosophers were skeptical of democracy as an effective political system.

They divided the region into seven kingdoms while the Romano-British population largely settled in Wales and Cornwall. The Anglo-Saxons had their own political practices, which included hereditary kings whose decisions were informed by a network of family and tribal advisers. The earliest known law code from Anglo-Saxon England was commissioned by King Ethelbert of Kent around 594. He combined Germanic traditions of financial restitution for crimes with Christian reverence for the primacy of the church in his kingdom.

Alfred the Great (r. 871–899), king of Wessex, united the English tribes against successive invasions by the Danes, and his grandson, Athelstan, went on to become the first king of all England in 927. By that time the role of king combined the primary roles of military leader and lawgiver. Although democracy did not exist in Anglo-Saxon England, the king's power was constrained by the *Witenagemot*, the Assembly of the Wise, which consisted of senior nobles and clergy who ratified treaties and drafted changes to the law. When the succession was in dispute, this assembly selected the next king, passing over women and children in favour of experienced military leaders who were already part of the Anglo-Saxon ruling hierarchy. When King Edward the Confessor died in 1066, the Witenagemot selected his brother-in-law, Harold Godwinson, as his successor over the claims of Edward's maternal cousin once removed, William, Duke of Normandy. William argued that Harold's succession was unlawful because Harold had sworn an oath to support William's claim to the throne. William raised an army in northwestern France and invaded England to seize the throne.

▶ A scene from the Bayeux Tapestry depicting William of Normandy's invasion of England in 1066.

King William I of England and his three successors. Clockwise from top: William I, William II, Stephen, Henry I.

William defeated Harold at the Battle of Hastings on October 14, 1066, and was crowned King William I of England. William did not present his claim as an act of conquest, but, rather, as one of lawful succession supported by the papacy. The claim that he was Edward's legitimate successor bound William and his successors to the legal and administrative framework of Anglo-Saxon England. In 1100, William's youngest son, Henry, declared on his coronation day that he would follow Anglo-Saxon legal precedents, including the freedom of the church, assessment of just inheritance taxes, and consultation with a council of his barons. Henry I's coronation charter became known as the Charter of Liberties, and future generations of barons and clergymen expected the king to obey the terms set down in this document.

Henry I's successors — his nephew, Stephen, and grandson, Henry II — both faced challenges to their claims to the throne. Their coronation charters helped persuade the church and nobility that they would uphold their traditional rights. Henry II, like his predecessors, frequently summoned councils of prominent barons and clergymen to discuss key legislation after he took the throne in 1154. Henry II also dispensed justice in person during his travels around England and his numerous possessions in what is now France. The England inherited by Henry II's sons, Richard I (r. 1189–1199) and John (r. 1199–1216) did not have a tradition of democracy, a concept that retained its association with social disorder, but there were accepted limits on the monarch's power. King John's eventual failure to uphold England's political and legal customs would become one of the reasons for the drafting of Magna Carta.

LIFE IN THIRTEENTH-CENTURY ENGLAND

The feudal system governed society during the reigns of King John and his immediate predecessors. The moral authority of the Roman Catholic Church supported this strict social order. The monarch was at the top of secular English society, above the barons who led lesser knights in battle and governed the peasants who worked on their lands. The church possessed its own social hierarchy of archbishops, bishops, parish priests, monks, and nuns, defending its independence from secular control by appealing disputes to the pope. Wealthy merchants and burgesses (townspeople) enjoyed a limited degree of self-government in the towns, as guaranteed by royal charters. There were two classes of peasants: the small percentage of "free" peasants, whose only authority was the king, and the *villeins*, or serfs, who were accountable to their social superiors, who owned the land that the serfs worked. At the time, English law defined freedom as "the natural power of every man to do as he pleases, unless forbidden by law or force"[1] and this freedom was elusive for serfs. Each manor had its own court for hearing disputes among the peasantry, operating as a microcosm of the state. From the reign of Henry II the landed nobility were also expected to attend royal courts

KING JOHN IN POPULAR CULTURE

There have been kings who have gone down in history as villains but received sympathetic treatment in modern popular culture. Richard III is both Shakespeare's villain and the misunderstood hero of numerous modern historical novels. In contrast, popular culture portrayals of King John over the centuries have been remarkably consistent. The king is not only a villain but a snivelling, cowardly, treacherous figure. In Shakespeare's *The Life and Death of King John*, the king orders the blinding of his nephew, Arthur, to ensure his grip on power. The 1938 film, *The Adventures of Robin Hood*, starring Errol Flynn, set the tone for all future Robin Hood films by showing John attempting to seize power through treachery while his brother, Richard, is detained on his way home from crusade. For many children, their first impression of John is the lion without a mane in the Walt Disney Productions 1973 animated film *Robin Hood* who sucks his thumb and complains that his mother always loved Richard best. Portrayals of John in popular culture are so villainous that they have been the subject of satire. In the 1993 Mel Brooks film *Robin Hood: Men in Tights*, a triumphant King Richard, standing before a cheering crowd, announces, "Brother, you have surrounded your given name with a foul stench! From this day forth, all the toilets in the kingdom shall be known as . . . johns!"

A medieval harvest field: two women bending forward reap with sickles. On the left is a bound sheaf while a man with a sickle in his belt prepares another for binding.

as the state assumed more control over the justice system. Knights served as jurors on county courts. This social structure resulted in the entire nobility possessing a working knowledge of common law and customs, which would inform the creation of Magna Carta in 1215.

The ruling Plantagenet dynasty, named for the broom plant (*planta genesta*) that was the emblem of Henry II's father, had a greater knowledge of the world outside England than the vast majority of their subjects. Henry II and his sons, Richard I and John, were not only kings of England, they presided over a vast empire that included all of England as well as the northern and western regions of what is now France: Normandy, Anjou, Maine, and Aquitaine. The monarchs moved throughout their empire to dispense justice, command the military, and exert their authority in person. The mobility of the royal court was also dictated by practical considerations. The

extensive royal household would exhaust the available food supply surrounding one castle and have to move on to the next residence. The court spoke Norman French, with Latin serving as a common language for Europe's clergymen, diplomats, lawgivers, and scholars.

The reigns of Henry II, Richard I, and John saw the formal division of the landed nobility into two distinct classes: there were the barons, some of whom held titles, who served the king directly, owned substantial tracts of land, and acted as military leaders; immediately below the barons were knights, who had the resources to equip themselves and participate in military campaigns or pay "shield money" in lieu of active service.[2] Over the course of the twelfth century, there were between seven and thirty "titled barons" — the earls who ranked directly below the king and his sons. The titled barons were the wealthiest of the hundred baronial families. These magnates controlled vast lands with twenty or thirty manors worked by serfs, enjoyed incomes of hundreds of pounds per year, lived in castles, and followed the trends in architecture, cuisine, and fashion set by the royal court.

By the thirteenth century, titled barons demonstrated their wealth and prestige by commissioning stone castles in place of separate timber buildings surrounded by stone walls, which was the predominant style of castle from 1066 until the thirteenth century. The barons enjoyed a diet rich in meats, including beef, mutton, pork, and poultry; Fridays and many Wednesdays were designated fast days on the church calendar when fish, such as sole, herring, or eels might be served. These fast days derived from Old Testament precedents and were intended to demonstrate piety and self-discipline. Raw produce was considered unhealthy, and fruits and vegetables were therefore confined to preserves and stews. The Angevin domains, the enormous collection of territories in western France controlled by the Plantagenet kings in the twelfth and thirteenth centuries, included the lucrative wine-producing regions of the Bordeaux and the Loire valleys; young wines stored in wooden casks were the favourite drinks of the aristocracy. John's wine cellar contained 180,000 gallons in 1201, though Philip II of France mocked John's inability to distinguish the best wines from inferior vintages.

One of England's first etiquette manuals was written around 1200. Titled *Urbanus Magnus* (*The Book of the Civilized Man*), it is filled with advice for those invited to a banquet in a lord of the manor's great hall during John's reign. The book contains many rules that are still recognized today, including instructions to keep elbows off the table and mouths closed while chewing food. The author, Daniel of Beccles, also provides advice that reflected his times, including instructions to look up at the ceiling while belching and to turn around to spit to avoid offending fellow diners. Men and women from baronial families wore floor-length garments to demonstrate that they did not do manual labour, and Henry II's choice to wear a shorter cloak earned him the nickname *curtmantle*, meaning "short robe."

As England's ruling class, the barons fiercely protected their traditional prerogatives, including the right to advise the king at council, govern their lands and peasants without interference, marry exclusively within their own class, and receive justice from their peers. While barons acted as administrators for the entire

The ruins of Wolvesey Castle in Winchester. The castle was the residence of the powerful bishops of Winchester during the twelfth century.

The medieval gatehouse in the town of Canterbury in Kent, England. Aside from London, most thirteenth-century English towns were small with only a few thousand inhabitants.

kingdom, lesser knights participated in the legislative process at a local level, bringing the records of county courts to the king's court. A recent study placed the number of knights at 3,453 during John's reign.[3] This number dropped over the course of the thirteenth century as inflation and advances in armour and weapons technology increased the cost of knighthood. By 1258, the cost of equipping a knight for battle might be a year's income from a modest estate; therefore, many poorer families dropped out of the knightly class. In contrast to the wealthy barons, a knight might possess a single fortified manor whose lands and peasant labour produced an income of ten pounds per year. Knighthoods provided a living for the younger sons of the baronial families. Inheritance in thirteenth-century England was governed by the rules of primogeniture, which passed estates intact to the eldest son. Daughters received their share of their family's wealth through their dowries while younger sons were equipped as knights or joined the clergy. Landless knights could attach themselves to a baronial household and provide military service. Despite the subordinate position of knights within the English ruling class, they were recognized as leaders of their communities. Knights served on juries, acted as county sheriffs, heard the appointments of attorneys, and brought local complaints to the king's court.

In contrast to the itinerant royal household, and those barons and knights who participated in continental military campaigns and crusades, the majority of John's subjects lived out their lives close to their birthplaces, rarely travelling beyond the nearest market town. As much as 90 percent of England's population in 1215 lived in the countryside, residing in villages and working on small farms on baronial estates.

In contrast to the meaty diet of the nobility, the rural peasantry lived predominantly on black bread, vegetable stews, and weak ale. Those who kept livestock sold most of their eggs and cheese at local markets to buy metal goods and salt. Even the poorest avoided drinking water because it was associated with diseases such as cholera and dysentery. A prosperous yeoman farmer might have a two-room timber-framed farmhouse that he shared with his family and livestock, but the majority of tenant farmers lived in one-room huts that could be moved around their tenements. Like the nobility, the peasantry passed their land holdings through primogeniture, and younger sons of peasant families were most likely to leave manorial farms and seek their freedom and fortune in the towns. A serf who resided in a town for a year and a day without being reclaimed by the lord of the manor became a free burgess. The majority of English towns were small. As late as the reign of John's grandson, Edward I, five out of six towns contained fewer than two thousand people,[4] most of whom lived in timber-framed houses. The exception was London. In 1199, Peter of Blois informed Pope Innocent III that London had 120 churches and forty thousand people, though modern historians place London's population at closer to half that number.

The temperate climate created by the medieval warm period of circa 900–1300 resulted in ample grain harvests and an expanding population. By the early thirteenth century, England contained just under three million inhabitants, while Scotland and Wales, whose people relied on animal husbandry instead of agriculture, each had a population of under half a million. The high infant mortality rate contributed to low average life expectancies.

King John hunting a stag with hounds. During John's reign, only the king had the right to hunt deer in England's forests.

Throughout the medieval period, the average life expectancy was around forty. Those who survived to adulthood could expect to live into their sixties if they did not fall victim to war, childbirth, or infectious disease. Nearly one-third of English land in 1215 consisted of forest where the king enjoyed a monopoly over all management and distribution of resources. Some of this land was forest in the modern sense of the word, including Sherwood Forest, associated with the legends of Robin Hood and his Merry Men, and the New Forest, which remains one of the largest tracts of woodland in England. Other thirteenth-century forests, however, consisted of inhabited countryside with villages and farmland. The rapidly expanding population resulted in demand for new villages and farmland in these regions, conditions that contributed to the reform of forest law in Magna Carta and the Charter of the Forest.

The regulations governing the use of forest land were extensive and arbitrary because the forest was both a hunting ground and a lucrative source of revenue for the king. William I and his descendants enforced a royal monopoly over hunting large animals in the forest. Members of the nobility could petition for a licence to hunt foxes, otters, badgers, and rabbits, but only the king, members of his hunting parties, or his foresters were entitled to hunt deer or wild boar. Penalties for poaching the king's game were severe. According to the Anglo-Saxon Chronicle, King William I "made many deer-parks; and he established laws therewith; so that whosoever slew a hart, or a hind, should be deprived of his eyesight. As he forbade men to kill the harts, so also the boars . . . His rich men bemoaned it, and the poor men shuddered at it." By the reign of Richard I, the punishment for killing a deer was blinding and mutilation.

The restrictions imposed by forest law went beyond hunting privileges. Permission from the king's chief forester was required before forest land could be cleared and cultivated, and the king received rent in perpetuity for these newly developed tracts. The right to pasture animals in the forest was strictly controlled and could be revoked at the king's discretion. Farmers could only chop down trees for their own use if the removal of a tree did not create waste, which was defined in the reign of Henry II as "If a man standing on the stump of an oak or other tree can see five other trees cut down around him." If an individual offender could not be identified in the forest courts, the chief forester had the power to impose a fine on the entire community.

"The law of the forest" was unpopular with the nobility, clergy, and peasantry alike because it prevented land development, impeded agriculture, and imposed fines on people of all social backgrounds. In 1209, the knight Roger de Crammaville of Kent was fined twenty marks for owning dogs that did not meet forest regulations, which dictated that three claws of their forepaws be removed to ensure that they were unable to hunt game. That same year, John ordered the destruction of unauthorized ditches and hedges on forest land. This decree resulted in wild animals — including deer, which had little fear of humans because of the harsh poaching laws — destroying crops in fields unprotected by hedges or ditches. In addition to collecting fines and other payments, John also used his forest prerogatives to settle personal scores. In 1200, he expressed his displeasure with the Cistercian Order by forbidding the monks from pasturing their livestock in the forest until twelve abbots begged his forgiveness on their knees.

A genealogical chart depicting Henry II and his eight children. John is in the bottom right corner.

John's conflict with the Cistercians reflected both his determination to assert the king's authority over the church and the expansion of religious orders over the course of the twelfth century. The expanding population resulted in more lay brothers available to work on monastery estates. As development of monastic lands increased, the activities of the religious orders came into conflict with forest law.

Everyone in John's England knew their place in the strict social hierarchy of the time. That included members of the royal household all the way down to the serfs bound to the manors of the landed nobility. The unique political circumstances of John's reign, including the expanding population and the conflicts between the king and his barons, would disrupt this social structure, culminating in the nobility imposing formal limits on the power of their king through Magna Carta. At the centre of this challenge to the social order was John, who remains one of the most controversial figures in English history.

THE MAKING OF KING JOHN

There have been recent attempts by historians to present John as an "underrated king."[5] These new interpretations of John's reign emphasize his attention to detail and energetic devotion to his royal duties. The decision by a group of powerful barons to first limit John's powers, then attempt to overthrow him when he repudiated

ENGLAND: THE NORMAN AND PLANTAGENET KINGS

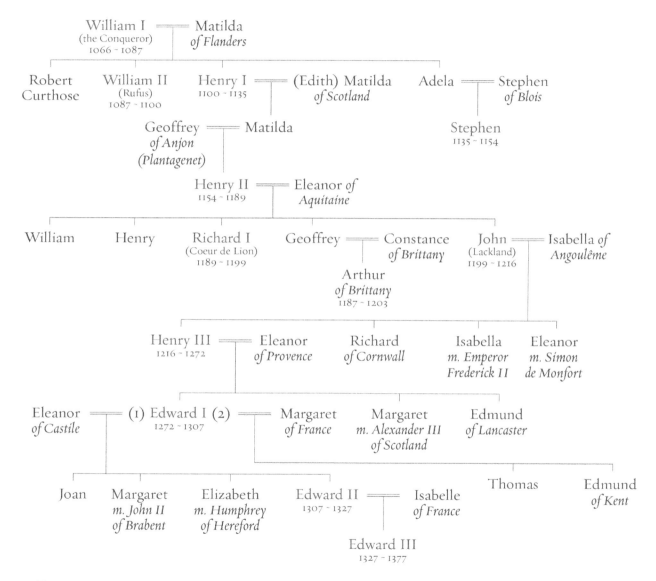

William I (the Conqueror) 1066 ~ 1087 ═══ Matilda *of Flanders*

Robert Curthose

William II (Rufus) 1087 ~ 1100

Henry I 1100 ~ 1135 ═══ (Edith) Matilda *of Scotland*

Adela ═══ Stephen *of Blois*

Geoffrey *of Anjon (Plantagenet)* ═══ Matilda

Stephen 1135 ~ 1154

Henry II 1154 ~ 1189 ═══ Eleanor *of Aquitaine*

William

Henry

Richard I (Coeur de Lion) 1189 ~ 1199

Geoffrey ═══ Constance *of Brittany*

John (Lackland) 1199 ~ 1216 ═══ Isabella *of Angoulême*

Arthur *of Brittany* 1187 ~ 1203

Henry III 1216 ~ 1272 ═══ Eleanor *of Provence*

Richard *of Cornwall*

Isabella *m. Emperor Frederick II*

Eleanor *m. Simon de Monfort*

Eleanor *of Castile* ═══ (1) Edward I (2) 1272 ~ 1307 ═══ Margaret *of France*

Margaret *m. Alexander III of Scotland*

Edmund *of Lancaster*

Joan

Margaret *m. John II of Brabent*

Elizabeth *m. Humphrey of Hereford*

Edward II 1307 ~ 1327 ═══ Isabelle *of France*

Thomas

Edmund *of Kent*

Edward III 1327 ~ 1377

❧ Plantagenet family tree.

Magna Carta, however, demonstrates his failure to fulfill the requirements of medieval kingship, including effective military leadership and consistent enforcement of the traditional laws and customs of his realm. King John's formative years were defined by the conflicts within his family. As the youngest of the eight children of King Henry II of England and his queen, Eleanor of Aquitaine, John did not grow up expecting to be king. He was born on December 24, 1166, and likely named in honour of the feast day of St. John the Evangelist, which fell three days after his birth. At the time of John's birth, Eleanor was over forty and his arrival was probably a surprise to his parents, who already had plans to divide their vast Anglo-French Angevin domains between their three elder surviving sons, Henry, Richard, and Geoffrey. The young Henry would receive his father's inheritance of England, Normandy, and Anjou; Richard would receive his mother's lands in Aquitaine; and Geoffrey would marry Constance, heiress to Brittany, and gain her lands. From a young age, John was therefore known as *Jean sans terre* or John Lackland. John and his sister, Joan, spent their early childhood at Fontevraud Abbey in Anjou, and Henry and Eleanor may have initially intended for their landless youngest son to enter the church. After leaving the abbey at age six, John continued his education with tutors in the household of his eldest brother, young Henry. As a result of his education, John was better educated than most laymen of his time; as king it was common for him to travel with a personal library.

ヽ Fontevraud Abbey, where King John spent his early childhood.

ヽ Canterbury Cathedral, the site of Thomas Becket's murder and Henry II's penance.

Henry II's determination to ensure that his youngest son received a share of the Angevin domains, despite the inheritance customs of the time, brought John's interests into conflict with those of his mother and older brothers from a young age. In the early 1170s, Henry II decided to remove three castles from young Henry's inheritance and give them to John on the occasion of his betrothal to Alicia of Savoy. At the time of these negotiations, Henry II was extremely unpopular with the barons and clergy because of his conflict with Thomas Becket, the archbishop of Canterbury, which had ended with the archbishop's murder by four knights in Canterbury Cathedral in 1170. Henry was also in conflict with his family because of his interference in

Eleanor's governance of her domains in Aquitaine and his refusal to allow his three oldest sons to have influence over his administration. In 1173–74, at the age of eighteen, young Henry led the Revolt of the Eaglets against his father, with support from his mother and brothers, senior barons, and the kings of France and Scotland. Henry II's superior military experience ultimately led to him defeating the uprising.

Henry II made efforts to repair his relationship with the church by doing penance for his role in Becket's death. On July 12, 1174, Henry II walked barefoot to Becket's tomb in the crypt, receiving lashes from the monks. This act was a public reconciliation of king and church. When the king's forces captured King William

▶ Chinon Castle was a favourite residence of Henry II, who died there in 1189.

the Lion of Scotland the next day, the victory therefore appeared to be divine providence. Like king and church, Henry II and his sons were publicly reconciled. The revolt was blamed on young Henry's advisers. John's mother, Eleanor, however, was not forgiven by her husband for her support of her sons, and she spent the rest of Henry II's reign imprisoned in a series of castles, playing little part in John's early life.

The reconciliation of Henry II and his sons in 1174, and the death of Alicia of Savoy in 1178, meant that a new role had to be found for John. When young Henry died of dysentery in 1183, the king expected Richard, now heir to the English throne, to cede Aquitaine to John. Richard refused, prompting John's first military campaign, an invasion of Aquitaine with the support of his father and brother, Geoffrey, that ended in a stalemate in 1184. With John's prospects in Aquitaine uncertain, Henry II decided that Ireland would be the place where his youngest son would make his fortune and wield political influence. John travelled there as Lord of Ireland in April 1185 at the age of nineteen. From the moment of his arrival in Waterford, however, John made a poor impression on the local Irish leaders.

The young Lord of Ireland mocked the appearance and customs of the Gaelic chieftains, pulled their beards, and showed himself to be "a mere youth, with an entourage

THE WIDER WORLD IN 1215

The known world for the English in 1215 was certainly not the entire world. In central Asia, Genghis Khan was building a vast Mongol Empire. The same year as Magna Carta, Genghis captured modern-day Beijing in the Battle of Zhongdu, following a two-year siege, gaining control of northern China. Contact between Western Europe and the Mongol Empire would not occur until the reign of John's son, Henry III, when the papacy unsuccessfully called for the Mongols to convert to Christianity and devote their military might to the crusades.

The possibility of lands across the Atlantic Ocean or south of the equator had been a subject of speculation by European scholars and clergymen since the eleventh century. German missionaries who travelled north to Scandinavia to convert the Vikings heard sagas of past expeditions to Vinland (modern-day Newfoundland). The eleventh-century German chronicler Adam of Bremen believed that Vinland was the only land to the west, across the Atlantic. "[V]ines producing excellent wine grow wild," he observed, "but beyond that island no habitable land is found in the ocean, every place beyond it is full of impenetrable ice and intense darkness." Europeans were unaware of the other lands and civilizations in the Americas, including the Mayan Empire, which was in decline after an eleventh-century period of drought, and the Mexica, who founded Tenochtitlan on the site of what is now Mexico City around the year 1200.

The English scholar Alexander of Neckam, whose mother, Hodierna, had nursed the future king Richard, speculated that there might be Antipodean people living "beneath our feet." Alexander was pessimistic about Europeans ever contacting these people because Aristotle believed that ships could not sail across the equator due to his belief that the intense heat of this region would make travel from the northern to southern hemisphere impossible.

composed only of youths, a stripling who listened only to youthful advice."[6] John's frivolity and disrespect attracted criticism as he travelled from Waterford to Dublin. He proved a poor administrator. He may have spent funds provided by Henry for military campaigns on lavish entertainments for his household. John demonstrated some interest in fulfilling his duties as Lord of Ireland, establishing several castles and providing land grants for royal administrators, but his administration there was judged to be a failure by his contemporaries and subsequent historians because of his reckless spending and poor relations with the local elites.

The royal party departed for England in December 1185 after only eight months in Ireland. Despite John's failures in Ireland, there is circumstantial evidence that Henry considered leaving the Angevin domains to him instead of Richard, who represented Eleanor's interests. The uncertainty Henry introduced into the succession may have been an attempt to control his eldest surviving son, who remained

◀ Statue of John's elder brother, Richard I "the Lionhearted," outside the Houses of Parliament, Westminster.

in conflict with his father. When it became clear in 1189 that Henry was dying and that Richard would be his undisputed successor, John joined forces with his elder brother against his father to gain the favour of the next king. John acquired a reputation for disloyalty by leaving his father's deathbed. Henry II died on July 6, 1189, at the fortified château de Chinon in Anjou in western France, cursing the faithlessness of his sons.

John, twenty-three at the time of Richard's ascension to the English throne, was nine years his brother's junior and only five feet, five inches tall. In contrast, Richard, at six-five, towered over his unimposing younger brother. John resembled his father, Henry II, in both appearance and temperament. He had curly red hair and a barrel-chested physique that became overweight as he grew older. Also like his father and numerous other members of the Plantagenet dynasty, he was prone to sudden changes in mood. Contemporaries observed that John could change from generous, hospitable, and good-natured to angry and vengeful in an instant, erupting into violent rages similar to those of Henry II. While Richard was a formidable soldier, John had neglected the martial training that was an essential part of any young nobleman's education, preferring hunting, hawking, music, and gambling. John also took unusual care with his appearance, enjoying sumptuous clothing and jewels, especially gold. In an era when rules for monastic orders prescribed two to four baths per year for monks and even the rich viewed bathing as a rare luxury, John took a bath every three weeks. John's formative experiences in a family where his parents and brothers were frequently at war with each other appear to have made him secretive, and he became skilled at dissimulation.

Despite their differences, the two brothers presented a united front during the early months of Richard I's reign. Richard released their mother, Eleanor, from confinement and she became a familiar and prominent figure at his court. John accompanied Richard to England for his coronation in August 1189 and was showered with lands, wealth, and honours. On August 29, John married Isabelle of Gloucester, whose married elder sisters were conveniently disinherited by the crown so that the earldom of Gloucester would pass to the king's brother. Richard named John the Count of Mortain, Normandy. The new king also confirmed John's right to the English castles that he had been granted by Henry II and bestowed new honours upon him, including the earldom of Cornwall. The revenues from John's six English shires alone provided him with an independent annual income of £4,000, making him one of the wealthiest men in England, and he maintained a large household in his capacity as Lord of Ireland.

Richard's accession brought John astonishing new wealth and prestige, but the king was careful to exclude him from any real position of power. There is evidence that Richard was well aware of his younger brother's limitations as a soldier and statesman, commenting to Roger of Howden in 1193, "My brother John is not the man to conquer a country if there is a single person able to make the slightest resistance to his attempts."

Richard departed his domains for the Third Crusade in 1190 and, as the only other adult male member of the ruling dynasty, John may have expected to be entrusted with a senior role in the governance of the Angevin domains. Instead, Richard entrusted England to his chief minister, Guillaume de Longchamp, and insisted that

John swear an oath to stay away from the kingdom for three years. Eleanor of Aquitaine, who exerted far more political influence during Richard's reign than John, modified the oath to place John's exile from England at Longchamp's discretion, but the existence of any limits on his movements demonstrated the distrust behind the public expressions of unity. Richard also refused to choose John as his successor, instead naming their nephew, Arthur of Brittany, son of their late brother, Geoffrey, as heir to the throne.

Richard was captured by Duke Leopold of Austria on his way home from the crusade in 1192 because of his rumoured involvement in the murder of Leopold's cousin, Conrad of Montferrat. The duke presented his captive to Holy Roman Emperor Henry VI, who held him for ransom. John seized the opportunity to assert his authority over Richard's domains. While Eleanor raised the ransom for Richard's release, John swore fealty to Philip II for Richard's French domains and offered Henry VI a substantial sum to keep Richard in captivity. Eleanor's interests prevailed over those of her youngest son, and Richard returned to England in March 1194. In May, the two brothers were publicly reconciled, though Richard displayed his contempt for his brother by forgiving John with the words, "Do not be afraid, John. You are a child; you have got into bad company." Despite Richard's

condescending attitude, the prospect of being named heir to the throne instead of his young nephew, Arthur, ensured John's loyalty for the remainder of his brother's reign. On his deathbed, following a crossbow wound to the shoulder he received while besieging a castle held by a rebel baron in Aquitaine in 1199, Richard acknowledged his brother, John, as heir to all the Angevin domains. Finally — and improbably — the youngest and oft-ignored son once known as John Lackland had begun his controversial reign as king of England.

John's upbringing and rivalry with Richard are crucial to understanding his conflicts with his barons and the church during his reign, circumstances that precipitated Magna Carta. From a young age, John became skilled in dissimulation and exploiting conflict within the ruling family for his own personal gain. During Richard's reign, John was quick to betray his brother or reconcile with him according to his self-interest. John's dissimulation continued after he became king. By 1215, the year of Magna Carta, a significant proportion of John's barons came to the conclusion that the king could not be trusted to keep his word and observe the customs of the realm outlined in the coronation charters of previous monarchs. The solution was Magna Carta, a formal charter of liberties imposed on the king by his subjects.

▸ Nineteenth-century engraving depicting King John refusing to accept the Magna Carta when it was first presented to him by his rebel barons.

Part 2
Magna Carta and the Charter of the Forest

Magna Carta and the subsequent Charter of the Forest (Carta de Foresta) were responses to the unique political, social, and economic circumstances that emerged during the reigns of King John and his son, King Henry III, including military defeats that ended Angevin control of western France, a multi-year break with the papacy and arbitrary treatment of influential barons. In 1215, neither John nor his barons expected the terms of Magna Carta to be respected for long. John repudiated the document within weeks and went to war with his barons. Only John's untimely death in 1216 provided the opportunity for the terms of Magna Carta to be entrenched and expanded through additional charters such as the Charter of the Forest during the reign of his son. Like John, Henry III had experienced military defeats and treated his barons arbitrarily, demonstrating the need for further charters and institutions to ensure the monarch followed the accepted law of the land. In the reign of Henry III, Magna Carta informed the emergence of parliamentary government.

THE REIGN OF KING JOHN AND THE COMING OF MAGNA CARTA

Like those of many of his predecessors, John's accession to the English throne was contested. Although Richard apparently acknowledged John as his successor to all his territories on his deathbed, the new king faced an immediate challenge from supporters of his twelve-year-old nephew, Arthur of Brittany. Anjou, Maine, Touraine, and Brittany supported Arthur as Richard's rightful heir to the Angevin domains; John had the support of England and Normandy. Arthur also had a powerful supporter in King Philip II of France.

Despite John's reputation for political and military incompetence, which dated from his time in Ireland and attempts to rebel against Richard, he began his reign with victories. When the teenage Arthur besieged his grandmother, Eleanor of Aquitaine, in the château de Mirebeau in 1202, John took decisive action to relieve the siege and defeat Arthur's forces.

The interior of Bordeaux Cathedral where King John married his second wife, Isabelle of Angouleme, in 1200.

Arthur was captured by John's barons on August 1, 1202, and imprisoned in the château de Falaise under the guardianship of William de Braose.

For John's barons, the existence of an alternate claimant to the throne was advantageous because they could threaten to shift their allegiance if the king disregarded the laws and customs of the kingdom. The barons expected John to come to terms with the captured Arthur as Henry II had come to terms with his three elder sons in 1174. Instead, John had the young man killed, and may even have done the deed himself. According to the Annals of Margam, a historical chronicle maintained by the Cistercian monks of Margam Abbey in Wales, "After King John had captured Arthur and kept him alive in prison for some time, at length, in the castle of Rouen, after dinner on the Thursday before Easter, when he was drunk and possessed by the devil, he slew him with his own hand, and tying a heavy stone to the body cast it into the river Seine."[7] There was no official announcement regarding Arthur's fate. He simply disappeared, allowing rumours of John's involvement to spread widely throughout his domains. John's assumed involvement in the disappearance of his nephew was a grave transgression, which cast a shadow over the king's reputation for the rest of his reign.

John's reputation deteriorated further when he was excommunicated from the Roman Catholic Church in 1209. John's predecessors, Henry I, Stephen, and Henry II, all experienced jurisdictional conflicts with the church, but John's inability to make peace with the papacy until the very end of his reign cemented a reputation for both villainy and arbitrary rule. The trouble began when the archbishop of Canterbury died in

1205. John seized the opportunity to appoint one of his staunch supporters, John de Gray, the bishop of Norwich, as the new archbishop of Canterbury. The Chapter of Canterbury Cathedral — the clerics who advised the late archbishop — however, claimed it was their right to elect the successor, which was accorded to the church by Henry I's Charter of Liberties. The chapter elected as archbishop one of their sub-priors, Reginald, who travelled to Rome for confirmation of his new position over John's objections.

The pope settled the dispute by advancing Stephen Langton, one of the eventual authors of Magna Carta, as his own candidate, dismissing the claims of the candidates chosen by both John and the chapter. John objected to Langton, both personally, because of his connections to Philip II's court in Paris, and because of the process by which he was chosen as archbishop. When John refused to allow Langton to enter England, let alone take up the role of archbishop of Canterbury, the pope placed England under interdict, forbidding most religious ceremonies to be performed throughout John's kingdom. John treated the interdict as a papal declaration of war and began confiscating lands from clergymen and religious communities who obeyed the pope over the king, circumstances that contributed to his eventual excommunication.

In addition to his treatment of his nephew and conflict with the church, John acquired a reputation for erratic treatment of his barons and personal villainy. John's second wife, Isabelle of Angouleme, was betrothed to one of his vassals, Hugh de Lusignan, before the king decided to marry the twelve-year-old heiress himself. John levied extraordinary taxes and demands for military service in his campaigns against Philip II to preserve his continental empire. Widows and orphans of barons were married against their will to John's closest allies.

While previous kings had taken mistresses, John became notorious for targeting the wives and daughters of his barons, in violation of his responsibilities as liege lord to the nobility. One monastic chronicler accused John of neglecting the affairs of state to remain in bed until noon with his young queen. The king developed a reputation for choosing pleasure over statecraft, an image bolstered by his love of fine clothes and jewels.

All of John's political, religious, and personal transgressions might have been tolerated by his subjects if he had achieved military victories that brought wealth and prestige to his barons and knights. Instead, John lived up to his childhood nickname of Lackland by losing most of his continental lands to Philip II. Philip seized Anjou in 1203 when John refused to accept the king of France as liege lord for the county. After Eleanor of Aquitaine died in 1204, one of her sons-in-law, King Alfonso VIII of Castile, took the opportunity to occupy part of her lands in the duchy of Aquitaine. In July 1214, the year before Magna Carta, John lost a pair of decisive battles that cost him most of his empire on the continent. After these defeats, John had to recognize Philip's territorial gains, agree to a six-year truce, and pay compensation. Barons who owned estates in both England and Normandy lost lands, and merchants engaged in continental trade found their ships seized by the French.

These military and economic disasters were the final straw for an influential group of John's barons led by Robert Fitzwalter of Little Dunmow, Essex. Fitzwalter

↖ Nineteenth-century French illustration of the Battle of Bouvines in 1214, which cost King John much of his territory in what is now France.

There were numerous barons and clergymen involved in the creation of Magna Carta, but the primary author appears to have been Stephen Langton, archbishop of Canterbury, whom John finally allowed to return to England in 1213 in an attempt to alleviate the discontent. Langton's first act upon his return was to issue an oath to the king that he would uphold the terms of Henry I's coronation charter, an oath John first accepted, then repudiated almost immediately. Langton's belief in the primacy of this coronation charter informed the creation of Magna Carta, which mirrored numerous terms from the earlier document, including freedom of the church, inheritance rights for the nobility, freedom from forced marriage for noble widows, and the separation of legal judgments from the financial needs of the monarch. Langton was a prolific writer who wrote commentaries on the Old Testament and established the modern organization of the Bible into chapters. Langton had also spent years travelling in Europe and would have been aware of continental precedents for rulers accepting limitations on their powers. Langton's leadership position with the church, long history of conflict with John, and knowledge of both English coronation charters and European precedents informed his leading role in the creation of Magna Carta.

described himself as "Marshall of the Army of God and Holy Church" and became leader of a party of twenty-five of his fellow barons who became known as the Northerners. As a faction, the rebel barons commanded the support of twelve hundred knights, with the most powerful baron leading two hundred knights and the least powerful commanding ten. These barons publicly repudiated their oaths of allegiance to John in May 1215, and their supporters seized control of the city of London, where Fitzwalter was Constable of Baynard's Castle. By June 1215, John had to accept that even the king was not above the laws and customs of his subjects.

With the loss of London and support for the rebel barons growing, John reluctantly agreed to limit his own powers and obey the precedents of his forbears by affixing his seal to Magna Carta at Runnymede Meadow, neutral ground near Windsor Castle, on June 15, 1215. The charter had the support of the Northerner faction of barons led by Fitzwalter, a dozen bishops, including Langton, and twenty abbots.

Llewelyn ap Iorwerth, Prince of Wales, and King Alexander II of Scotland also supported the new charter. None of these figures saw the charter as a revolutionary document that would disrupt the strict social hierarchy of early thirteenth-century England but as an affirmation of existing customs and laws codified in the coronation charters of Henry I and Henry II. While the rebels did not intend to be revolutionaries, the creation of the charter set a new legal precedent. John was the first English king to accept terms drafted by his subjects, proving that nobody, not even the monarch, was above the law of the land.

THE KEY PRINCIPLES OF MAGNA CARTA

Archbishop Langton and the rebel barons arranged the terms of the charter in the order that reflected the social hierarchy of the thirteenth century and the structure of past coronation charters. Magna Carta begins with the clause guaranteeing freedom of the church to govern its own internal affairs, followed by the terms outlining the inheritance prerogatives of the nobility. Reform to forest law, local administration, and rights to urban merchants came after rights for the elites. There are terms that reflected the political and economic circumstances of 1215, including the names of corrupt local officials to be removed from office and the release of Welsh and Scottish hostages. Not until clauses 39 and 40 of the sixty-three in the charter does Magna Carta define justice and equality before the law in the manner that resonates to the

present day. While these terms were not the most important for the authors of Magna Carta, they are the rights codified in the charter that remained important to future generations. Today, Magna Carta is best known for certain key principles: affirming that no one — even the king — is above the law of the land, the right to due process, and the right to trial by one's peers. The charter also provides a precedent for freedom from forced marriage.

Key Principle: Nobody Is Above the Law of the Land

The concluding sections of Magna Carta emphasize the king's accountability to the laws and customs of England, mandating outside scrutiny of the king's appointments and decisions. Under pressure from the rebel barons, John agreed in clause 61, "wishing these things to be enjoyed fully and undisturbed in perpetuity, we give and grant the following security: namely, that the barons shall choose any twenty-five barons of the realm they wish, who with all their might are to observe, maintain and cause to be observed the peace and liberties which we have granted and confirmed to them by this our present charter. . ." Previous monarchs had agreed to consult the senior barons and clergy before making key decisions, but Magna Carta introduced outside checks and balances on the monarch's power. If four of the twenty-five barons learned of an offence committed by one of the king's bailiffs or sheriffs, the entire council of barons had the right to make amends by "seizing castles lands and possessions, and in such other ways as they can, saving our

A king dictating the law to a scribe, with three clerics and a soldier.

person and those of the queen and our children, until in their judgment, amends have been made . . ." The system of checks and balances placed the monarch within the legal framework of his kingdom instead of above the law of the land.

Although the barons presented themselves as defenders of traditional rights and customs, their demands in the charter had the potential to upset the social hierarchy of the period, allowing a king's vassals to confiscate parts of his revenue if he did not fulfill his obligations. Within weeks of signing the charter, John had second thoughts. Deeply upset at having been challenged and determined to recover his undisputed position at the apex of English government and society, he sought to be absolved from his oath to uphold Magna Carta. After more than a decade of conflict with the papacy, John reconciled with Pope Innocent III who released him from his oath. Conversely, the principle that nobody, not even the monarch, was above the law of the land allowed Magna Carta to transcend the specific political climate of 1215 and inspire legislative reform for centuries to come. The seventeenth-century jurist Sir Edward Coke, who was responsible for the modern revival of interest in the principles codified by Magna Carta, declared "Magna Charta is such a fellow that he will have no 'Sovereign.'" As will be discussed in part 3, Coke's interpretation of Magna Carta inspired both the Petition of Right, which constrained the powers of King Charles I prior to the outbreak of the English Civil Wars, and the American Bill of Rights. The principle that nobody, not even the monarch, is above the law of the land allowed Magna Carta to outlast the circumstances of 1215.

Key Principle: The Right to Due Process

The right to due process — that is, fair treatment from the judicial system that reflects established rules and principles — as described in the charter is one of the most famous sections of Magna Carta. It has reached the statute books of other countries in the English-speaking world such as Australia, New Zealand, and Canada. In both the Canadian Bill of Rights and the Charter of Rights and Freedoms, the term for due process is *fundamental justice*, the procedural rights to be expected when facing a judicial process. In the United States, the Fifth and Fourteenth Amendments of the Constitution contain due process clauses developing ideas that were first codified in Magna Carta.

Clause 29 of the 1297 version of Magna Carta, which remains on the British statute books to the present day (Clause 39 in 1215), states, "No Freeman shall be taken or imprisoned, or be disseised of his Freehold, or Liberties, or free Customs, or be outlawed, or exiled, or any other wise destroyed; nor will. We not pass upon him, nor condemn him, but by lawful judgment of his Peers, or by the Law of the land. We will sell to no man, we will not deny or defer to any man either Justice or Right." The language goes beyond the political circumstances of the early thirteenth century because it refers to "freemen" instead of a specific social class of the period such as barons, knights, or clergymen. When the feudal system ultimately broke down in the late Middle

▶ "King John's Castle" in Limerick, Ireland. As Lord of Ireland, King John acquired a reputation for misrule.

Ages, the number of freemen soared, allowing this principle to expand until it became a universal right.

For the supporters of Magna Carta in 1215, however, the right to due process was an essential constraint on the king's power. Over the course of his reign, John had confiscated lands, wealth, and titles from barons and knights who displeased him without any semblance of due process. The most notorious example of the king's arbitrary behaviour was the destruction of the wealthy de Braose family.

At the time of John's ascension in 1199, William de Braose, fourth Lord of Bramber, was one of the wealthiest barons in the kingdom, controlling vast estates in Wales and Ireland. William was also one of the new king's closest confidants, trusted with the guardianship of the rival claimant to the throne, Arthur of Brittany, after he was apprehended by John's supporters. Following Arthur's disappearance, William continued to rise in the king's service, gaining the right to keep any land he conquered in Wales in addition to his lordship of Limerick in Ireland.

Relations between John and William deteriorated around 1208 because of a financial dispute. William owed a substantial debt to the treasury, and the king demanded that he send his eldest son to court as a hostage until the funds were repaid. In response, William's wife, Maude, declared, "She would not deliver her children to a king who had murdered his own nephew." Since William had been one of the last people to see Arthur alive, her accusation was credible and further undermined the king's reputation. Maude immediately realized her mistake and sent a gift of cattle from the de Braose lands to Queen Isabelle, hoping that she would intercede with the king on the family's behalf.

Maude's attempts to make amends were unsuccessful. John was enraged and seized William's lands along the Welsh border. The conflict with the de Braose family was more than a personal dispute. The king utilized the full machinery of the state to settle his score with the Braoses. The royal exchequer claimed all William's assets, and John personally led troops to Wales to seize the de Braose castles. When William sought the assistance of John's son-in-law, Llewelyn ap Iorwerth, Prince of Wales, he was branded a traitor by the king, worsening his family's prospects further.

While William gathered allies in Wales, John's soldiers pursued his family to Ireland, where Maude and her son were arrested. A desperate Maude offered the king larger and larger sums of money for the release of herself and her son and the return of William's lands and positions. John accepted a promise to pay more than £33,000 — an outrageous sum that was higher than his own annual income. When William and Maude were inevitably unable to pay, the de Braose family was outlawed, a condition that deprived them of any benefit or protection under the laws of the land. William fled to France disguised as a beggar, but Maude and her son were imprisoned in Corfe Castle in 1210 and starved to death on the king's orders in one of the dungeons.

John denied any claim that he had violated established laws and customs, writing that he had acted "according to the custom of our realm and the law of the exchequer." John's barons, however, were horrified by the king's destruction of the de Braose family over an unpaid debt and an indiscreet remark. The right to due process enshrined in Magna Carta was intended to prevent other noble families from becoming the target of the king's wrath in the manner of William and Maude de Braose.

Key Principle: The Right to Judgment by One's Peers

The same clause of Magna Carta that enshrined the right to due process also promised a form of trial by jury, stating in the 1297 versions "nor will We not pass upon him, nor condemn him, but by lawful judgment of his Peers, or by the Law of the land." Like the right to due process, the right to be judged by a jury of peers is language that inspired legal reform for centuries while being firmly rooted in the political circumstances of John's reign. The king's disproportionate response to offences committed by the de Braose family and the presumed murder of his nephew demonstrated that he was willing to ignore established laws and customs to settle personal scores. Magna Carta addressed this by codifying the custom of trial by jury.

As England's ruling class, John's barons expected to resolve disputes among themselves. John's predecessors recognized that the barons expected judgments in keeping with existing customs accepted by the entire English nobility. Henry I's coronation Charter of Liberties made clear that justice was not at the discretion of the king alone, stating, "If any of my barons or men commit a crime, he shall not bind himself to a payment at the king's mercy as he has been doing in the time of my father or my brother; but he shall make amends according to the extent of the crime as he would have done before the time of my father in the time of my other predecessors."

As early as 1100, justice was supposed to be formally separated from the financial interests of the monarch.

The reference to Henry I's "other predecessors," the Saxon kings who reigned before the Norman Conquest, may refer to pre-1066 legal charters such as the Law of Ethelbert, which emphasized the compensation that victims of a crime should receive from the perpetrators rather than at the monarch's discretion. Henry I separated "treachery or heinous crime" from this restorative framework of perpetrators compensating their victims, but issues between barons such as property disputes and assaults could be settled among themselves.

↘ Henry I holding his coronation charter, which set precedents for Magna Carta.

Henry II's centralization of England's justice system, from local manorial courts run by the nobility to courts directly controlled by the king that had jurisdiction over the whole kingdom, introduced a jury of presentment or indictment. The 1166 Assize of Clarendon established this grand jury and began the process of instituting an evidence-based model for deciding guilt or innocence, moving away from previous methods of settling scores, including trial by ordeal or trial by battle. This evolution was a gradual one: trial by ordeal is mentioned in the assize and the possibility of trial by battle remained on British statute books until 1819. Nevertheless, the assize, called for the creation of a grand jury, declaring, "King Henry has ordained on the advice of all his barons, for preserving peace and maintaining justice that inquiry be made through the several counties and through several hundreds by twelve of the more lawful men of the hundred and by four of the more lawful men of each [township], upon oath that they will tell the truth, whether in their hundred or in their [township] there is any man accused or said to be a robber or a murderer . . ." By 1175, Henry II had authorized itinerant judges to dispense the king's justice throughout his kingdom, a reform that was unpopular because it interfered with local manorial or county courts and was seen as an opportunity for the monarch to collect additional revenue through fines.

The itinerant judges were authorized to assemble local juries from regional nobility. Formal legal education was not available until around 1250, but a working knowledge of the law was an essential skill for the entire English upper class from the most powerful titled barons to the county knights in their service. Even landless knights might be called upon to serve on local juries and adjudicate disputes. Despite Henry II's efforts at centralization, manorial and village courts traditionally enjoyed a great deal of autonomy because the king was rarely in England to take charge of the legal system himself.

The autonomy of the English barons over judicial matters was threatened by John's loss of most of the Angevin domains, which resulted in the king spending much of his reign based in England. John's urgent need for funds to recover his continental possessions meant that his judgments on baronial property disputes and marriage alliances were influenced by bribery and extortion. Trial by jury was a means of separating the justice system from the king's immediate needs and developing consistency of law and custom between reigns. John's arbitrary rule ignored centuries of legal reforms codified by Henry I and Henry II. Magna Carta's codification of trial by jury attempted to end this regression and continue the process of separating justice from the financial interests of the monarch.

Key Principle: Freedom from Forced Marriage

Magna Carta is one of the key documents to bridge the divide between the status of women in medieval England and the twenty-first century. The intent of Magna Carta clauses pertaining to women was to reinforce the status of the nobility as a distinct social group and to ensure that children from first marriages did not lose their inheritances when their widowed mother remarried. Nevertheless, the formal recognition of distinct privileges enjoyed by widowed noblewomen set a precedent for future legislation guaranteeing the rights of women.

▼ Funerary monuments of King John's parents, King Henry II and Eleanor of Aquitaine, in Fontevraud Abbey. As Duchess of Aquitaine, Eleanor was one of the most powerful women of the twelfth century and chose Henry as her second husband.

Women occupied a subordinate place in the medieval social hierarchy that transcended their social status. While a man enjoyed greater autonomy if he was a baron instead of a peasant, high social status for a woman meant that her marriage was the concern of her parents and, in certain cases, the king. While a peasant woman might delay marriage until she was in her twenties, the betrothals and marriages of royal and noble women were often arranged at the minimum age of twelve.

Once a medieval woman was married, her property, including her dowry, legally belonged to her husband. The bridegroom was expected to provide a marriage portion for the maintenance of his wife throughout her lifetime. Husband and wife also shared a legal identity, rendering married women unable to testify on their own behalf in court in most circumstances. Magna Carta upheld the inferior status of married women's testimony, stating, "No one shall be taken or imprisoned upon the appeal of a woman for the death of anyone except her husband."

The wives of kings were exempt from the coverture laws that determined the legal status of other married women. Matilda of Boulogne and Eleanor of Aquitaine, the respective queens of Stephen and Henry

II, administered their own domains and even organized military campaigns. Richard and John appeared to have reversed this trend by keeping their queens, Berengaria of Navarre and Isabelle of Angouleme, firmly in the background. Anglo-Saxon royal councils of prominent lords and clergy included the abbesses who governed convents, the most prominent women in the church hierarchy.

The largest group of autonomous women in thirteenth-century England were widowed noblewomen, and it was their freedom from forced marriage that was codified by Magna Carta. In contrast to maidens, who were expected to obey their parents and wives who owed obedience to their husbands, widows had the freedom to choose whether to remarry. Henry I's Charter of Liberties made this freedom from forced marriage explicit in 1100 when the king promised "If, on the death of her husband, the wife is left and without children, she shall have her dowry and right of marriage, and I will not give her to a husband unless according to her will."

For both Richard and John, the financial demands of their military campaigns often superseded the conventions of their roles as liege lords to widows and orphaned noblewomen. Both kings allowed wealthy members of the urban middle class to buy their way into the aristocracy by purchasing the ability to marry widows and orphans of knights in contravention of the social hierarchy of the period, confiscating the dowers of widows who refused to comply. Magna Carta forbade the practice of the king arranging marriages between nobles and their social inferiors, stating, "Heirs may be given in marriage, but not to someone of lower social standing. Before a marriage takes place, it shall be made known to

the heir's next-of-kin." The requirement to inform relatives of the marriage limited the king's ability to arrange an unequal marriage for one of his wards.

Regarding the specific protection of widows from forced marriages, Magna Carta stated, "No widow shall be compelled to marry, so long as she wishes to remain without a husband. But she must give security that she will not marry without royal consent, if she holds her lands of the Crown, or without the consent of whatever other lord she may hold them of." The king could withhold permission for what he considered to be an unsuitable marriage, preventing a wealthy widow from marrying one of his enemies, but he could not force a widow to marry. Widows were also guaranteed the use of their marriage portion and the right to remain in their marital home for forty days following her husband's death.

The Magna Carta clauses concerning marriage rights pertained to elite women alone. Nevertheless, the identification of clear legal rights for widows in 1215 set precedents for legislation in future centuries that allowed women freedom from forced marriage and control over their property.

THE REPUDIATION OF MAGNA CARTA AND THE DEATH OF KING JOHN

Magna Carta has gone down in history as one of the foundational documents of common law and human rights, but neither the barons nor John expected the charter to signify more than a temporary truce in 1215. Although John swore "that all these things shall be observed in good faith and without evil intent," the rebel barons knew that John had a long history of disregarding laws and customs that conflicted with his personal interests. Magna Carta imposed unprecedented limits on the monarch's prerogatives, and there seemed little possibility that John would adhere to the terms any longer than it was necessary to regain control of his kingdom. Within weeks of affixing his seal to Magna Carta, the king was searching for an opportunity to be released from the charter's terms.

Despite the skepticism on both sides regarding the long-term viability of the agreement, copies of Magna Carta, engrossed with the king's seal, were distributed to key castles, cathedrals, and towns throughout England.

The inclusion of clauses concerning Wales and Scotland (see sidebar page 53) suggests that Magna Carta travelled even farther afield in Britain. Each version of the charter was laboriously handwritten by clerks. Distribution took weeks, as the only means of transport were by horseback or riverboat. Since the literacy rate in medieval England may have been as low as 5 percent in rural areas, Magna Carta was read aloud in churches and town halls in French, Latin, and English.

The tenuous truce between John and the supporters of Magna Carta fell apart in a matter of months. After years of conflict with the church, John reconciled with the papacy, and the pope absolved the king

FORGOTTEN PEOPLE AND CLAUSES IN MAGNA CARTA

Magna Carta contains timeless principles that have shaped democracy, law, and human rights over the past eight hundred years, but the charter also contains clauses specific to the political and military circumstances of John's reign, which are little known today. The 1215 version of Magna Carta contains a list of families who were to be dismissed from their offices in government, including "Philip Mark with his nephew Geoffrey, and all their followers." Philip Mark was the High Sheriff of Nottinghamshire and Derbyshire and the Royal Forests and may have been a model for the sheriff of Nottingham in the Robin Hood legends.

Not all figures censured by the charter were English. In a society where local allegiances and kinship bonds held communities together, the foreign mercenaries imported to enforce John's decrees were especially unpopular. Magna Carta stated, "Immediately after the concluding peace, we will remove from the kingdom all alien knights, crossbowmen, sergeants and mercenary soldiers who have come with horses and arms to the hurt of the realm." The presence of foreign mercenaries in England threatened the leadership prerogatives of barons and knights in their communities.

The defence of English castles was addressed in Magna Carta. "No constable," it read, "is to compel any knight to give money for castle guard, if he is willing to perform that guard in his own person or by another reliable man . . ." Key clauses from Magna Carta are timeless and continue to be relevant today, but others demonstrate that it was also a product of the unique political circumstances of England in the early thirteenth century.

↖ The tomb of King John in Worcester Cathedral. When John died, his rebel barons transferred their allegiance from the future King Louis VIII of France to John's young son, Henry III.

from his oath to uphold Magna Carta. John's repudiation of the charter sparked the outbreak of the First Barons' War in the summer of 1215. The experiment of limiting the king's powers with a charter imposed by his subjects was temporarily abandoned in favour of the traditional method of challenging a medieval monarch's rule: supporting a rival candidate.

In the fall of 1215, the rebel barons under the leadership of Fitzwalter, with the support of the Scots and Welsh, sent envoys to Philip II's heir, the future king Louis VIII of France, asking him to invade England and establish himself as king. Louis had a distant blood claim to the English throne through his marriage to John's niece, Blanche of Castile, and the military resources to mount an invasion. The decision to invite a French prince to invade England attracted criticism in the centuries following Magna Carta. For example, William Shakespeare's play *The Life and Death of King John,* written in the 1590s, presented John in a villainous light because of his treatment of his nephew, Arthur, but also made the rebel barons appear traitorous because they transferred their allegiance to Louis.

In 1215, however, national boundaries were more fluid than they were in Shakespeare's time or today. William the Conqueror was the descendant of Norsemen who settled in the Duchy of Normandy, and yet he had successfully invaded England in 1066 and founded a new dynasty of English kings. During Henry II's reign, the king of England controlled more of modern-day France than the king of France, and there remained potential for John's successors to regain these lands. John's court spoke French. All of William I's successors until the reign of Edward I, with the exception of Henry I, married princesses from regions that now comprise France. Prior to the sixteenth-century Protestant Reformation, England and France were both Roman Catholic kingdoms, and the two royal courts shared numerous cultural similarities. In the thirteenth century, Louis appeared to be more of a regional power broker than a representative of a "foreign" kingdom.

Louis first sent knights to assist the barons in November 1215, then landed on the Isle of Thanet in eastern Kent at the head of an army on May 21, 1216. According to one chronicler, John was in no position to resist because "he did not have much trust in his own troops," which included French mercenaries.[8] Louis marched unopposed to London where he was proclaimed king in St. Paul's Cathedral, receiving the homage of Alexander II of Scotland and senior English barons. John was forced into retreat, reputedly losing the crown jewels when one of his baggage wagons overturned crossing an estuary in East Anglia.

Louis's invasion of England was ultimately thwarted by John's sudden death at Newark Castle on October 18, 1216, from dysentery that allegedly followed "a surfeit of peaches and cider."[9] John was so unpopular at the time that there were rumours he had been poisoned by a discontented monk. The accession of John's nine-year-old eldest son as Henry III changed the political landscape. Magna Carta specifically protected the inheritance rights of minors, stating, "If, however, the heir of any [of our earls and barons] has been under age and in wardship, when he comes of age he shall have his inheritance without relief or fine." Furthermore, the accession of the first child-king of England since 978 provided the opportunity for senior barons and clergymen to govern the country in Henry's name, reissue Magna Carta, and build upon the charter's clauses to institute further reforms.

Henry III was crowned king at Gloucester Cathedral on October 28, 1216, since Louis's occupation of London made it impossible for the coronation to take place in the traditional venue, Westminster Abbey. In the absence of the archbishops of Canterbury and York, he was crowned by the bishop of Winchester. John's widowed queen, Isabelle, provided one of her circlets to serve as the crown because of the loss of the crown jewels during the hostilities with the barons.

Despite the makeshift coronation, Henry III's government, led by William Marshall, first Earl of Pembroke, successfully persuaded senior barons to "defend our land" against Louis. Marshall's forces defeated the French at the Second Battle of Lincoln on May 20, 1217, and Louis was driven out of southwestern England. In September 1217, Marshall and Louis negotiated the Treaty of Lambeth, which marked the end of the First Barons' War. Louis agreed to relinquish his claim to the English throne and acknowledge Henry III in exchange for ten thousand marks. The French and Scottish troops departed from England. The peace allowed the barons and clergymen who comprised Henry III's government to resume the process of reform that began with Magna Carta.

THE CHARTER OF THE FOREST: PROTECTION OF THE COMMONS

Magna Carta promised to reform forest law, the complex and arbitrary ordinances that restricted development of crown lands. The charter decreed, "All evil customs of forest and warrens, foresters and warreners, sheriffs and their servants, river banks and their wardens are to be investigated at once in every county by twelve sworn knights of the same county who are to be chosen by worthy men of the county, and within forty days of the inquiry they are to be abolished. . . ." As discussed in the previous section, forest law was unpopular with people from a variety of social backgrounds from the barons who controlled vast estates to their peasant tenants. The rising population in thirteenth-century England made access to new agricultural and pastoral land a necessity and a third of the kingdom was designated "forest" under the direct control of the monarch.

Within months of the conclusion of the First Barons' War, the "evil customs" governing forest law in John's reign were defined and abolished by the underage Henry III's council in a new document: the Charter of the Forest. In contrast to Magna Carta, which primarily addressed the concerns of barons and knights with certain clauses pertaining to the church and urban merchants, the Charter of the Forest stated, "These liberties concerning the forests we have granted to everybody," acknowledging that the forests were the common concern of people from all social backgrounds. The Charter of the Forest set lasting precedents regarding community responsibility for the management and use of shared resources throughout the English-speaking world. The charter also set precedents regarding public access to crown land.

The Charter of the Forest acknowledged that deer remained the property of the king but abolished the physical punishments for poaching imposed by Henry III's predecessors since 1066. According to the charter, "No one shall henceforth lose life or limb because of our venison, but if anyone has been arrested and convicted of taking venison he shall be fined heavily if he has the means; and if he has not the means, he shall lie in our prison for a year and a day. . . ." Once again, the difference in penalties based on "means" revealed that the charter was intended to define forest law for everyone, rather than the nobility alone.

The Charter of the Forest precisely defined the "evil customs" mentioned in Magna Carta, and presented an alternative vision for the management of common resources. In contrast to the arbitrary regulations and fines imposed for forest offences by John and his predecessors, the charter stated that "Every free man may henceforth without being prosecuted make in his wood or in land he has in his forest, a mill, a preserve, a pond, a marl-pit or a ditch, or arable outside the covert in arable land, on condition that it does not harm any neighbour." This clause both revoked John's unpopular decrees and transferred authority over forest development from the king to the commons. Instead of answering to the king alone, forest dwellers had to consult with their communities, ensuring that any development did not disadvantage their neighbours.

The Charter of the Forest also ended the unpopular practice of monarchs arbitrarily transforming new land into "forest," stating that, "All woods made forest

↖ King John's eldest son, King Henry III, on his throne.

by King Richard our uncle or King John our father, up to the time of our first coronation shall be immediately disafforested." Although surviving evidence suggests that John only created two new forests during his reign, the arbitrary and mercenary nature of these changes infuriated his subjects and they were eager to ensure that Henry III and his successors did not exercise the same prerogatives.

The Charter of the Forest remains the statute in force for the longest period of time in England. Large game remained property of the Crown in law until the 1971 Wild Creatures and Forest Laws Act in the United Kingdom formally abolished "any prerogative right of Her Majesty to wild creatures . . . together with any prerogative right to set aside land or water for the breeding, support or taking of wild creatures; and any franchises of forest, free chase, park or free warren." In England, the New Forest and the Forest of the Dean still maintain special courts for adjudicating forest law as dictated by the Charter of the Forest.

THE PROVISIONS OF OXFORD AND THE DEVELOPMENT OF PARLIAMENT

Henry III's coming of age threatened to reverse all the reforms introduced by the barons during the first decade of his reign. The adult king was not obliged to honour legislation passed over the course of his minority, and there was concern among the reforming barons that he would repudiate Magna Carta and the Charter of the Forest because they constrained his ability to levy taxes to fund his building projects and continental wars. To the relief of the reformers, the adult Henry III reissued Magna Carta and the Charter of the Forest in 1225, in exchange for a fifteenth of the movable property of the clergy and a land tax on the towns. Between 1225 and his death in 1272, Henry III swore to uphold the terms of both Magna Carta and the Charter of the Forest nearly a dozen times.

In contrast to his father, John, Henry III was not viewed as a villain. He was a deeply religious man and an enthusiastic patron of art and architecture. His extensive building program included the Westminster Abbey that stands today, the Great Hall at Winchester Castle, and extensive renovations to Windsor Castle and the Tower of London. Henry was also a devoted husband to his queen, Eleanor of Provence, and was closely involved in the upbringing of his five children, including a daughter with special needs.

⬎ The Houses of Parliament in London. Magna Carta informed the development of parliament in England.

In the political realm, however, Henry's indecisiveness and willingness to be influenced by his favourites incurred the distrust of his barons. Like John, Henry was often dismissive of the grievances of his barons and ignored the provisions of Magna Carta when they conflicted with his own aims or those of his favourites. Barons in conflict with the king's favourites did not receive the justice dictated by the Great Charter. For example, in April 1258, John Fitzgeoffrey, Lord of Shere manor in Surrey, sought redress from the king when Aymer de Lusignan, bishop-elect of Winchester, sent armed men to Shere during a dispute, killing one of Fitzgeoffrey's servants. Since Lusignan was the king's half-brother, however, Fitzgeoffrey found that the king "did not wish to hear him" and made light of the dispute.

Barons discontented with Henry III's favouritism and arbitrary rule rallied around the leadership of his brother-in-law, Simon de Montfort, sixth Earl of Leicester. Although Simon was born in Montfort-l'Amaury, which is now a southwestern suburb of Paris, and was therefore as foreign as Henry III's favourites, his family had a long history of finding their interests in conflict with those of England's kings. When John lost Normandy to Philip II of France, he was unwilling to allow the Montfort family to keep their English earldom. John confiscated Leicester from Simon's father in 1207.

Simon saw Henry III's coming of age as an opportunity to regain the earldom. During the early 1230s, Simon travelled to England to swear homage to the king. At Henry's court, his intelligence, charisma, and political acumen made an immediate impression on the king and his barons and he became part of the monarch's inner circle, marrying the king's youngest sister, Eleanor, in 1238. Henry granted Simon the earldom of Leicester in 1239. As Earl of Leicester, the ambitious Simon found that the king's favouritism toward his half-siblings and their

Caernarfon Castle, site of modern-day investitures of Princes of Wales. King John's grandson, Edward I, commissioned the Castle during his conquest of Wales in 1283.

WALES AND SCOTLAND IN MAGNA CARTA

English barons and clergymen were not the only supporters of Magna Carta. The rulers of Wales and Scotland, Prince Llewelyn ap Iowerth (the Great) and King Alexander II, were also party to the charter, and their interests were directly addressed by a series of clauses at the end of the document. Both Llewelyn and Alexander had close political and personal ties to John. Llewelyn was married to John's illegitimate daughter, Joan, and accompanied his father-in-law on his Scottish campaign in 1209. Alexander was betrothed to one of John's legitimate daughters, also named Joan. Despite these family connections, John distrusted both men and kept hostages from both the Welsh and Scottish ruling families to ensure their obedience to his wishes.

Llewelyn and Alexander regarded Magna Carta as an opportunity to recover their imprisoned relatives and free themselves from fealty to John. They supported the rebel barons and were treated as fellow magnates in the charter. Magna Carta decreed that the Welsh would enjoy equal rights before the law to the English. "If we have disseised or deprived Welshmen of lands, liberties or other things without lawful judgement of their peers, in England or in Wales, they are to be returned to them at once . . ." Llewelyn's son and other Welsh hostages were to be returned to him. The supporters of Magna Carta viewed Alexander as having the legal rights of a fellow English baron concerning his relations with John. The charter guaranteed the return of his two sisters and other Scottish hostages. Magna Carta is one of the earliest examples of a charter addressing rights and privileges for all of Great Britain instead of a single kingdom.

Westminster Abbey as it stands today is the most famous of Henry III's numerous building projects.

supporters threatened his own interests. Simon became involved in a dispute over the lordship of Pembroke, which Eleanor claimed as part of her dower lands.

Simon became the leader of a faction of barons demanding lasting political change. On April 30, 1258, Simon and six other powerful barons, accompanied by dozens of knights, arrived at the great hall at Westminster to present the king with the terms that became known as the Provisions of Oxford after the location of the parliament that met in June of that same year. Simon and his supporters left their swords outside the hall, but they wore full armour, implying that they would use force if the king did not accept limits on his power. The Provisions of Oxford have been described as England's first constitution, and they were among the first government documents to be published in English as well as Latin and French, demonstrating that these political reforms were intended for a broad audience instead of the barons and senior clergy alone.

The Provisions of Oxford began with a demand for an elected judiciary that would guarantee the equality before the law promised by Magna Carta, stating, "It has been provided that from each county there shall be elected four discreet and lawful knights who, on every day that the county [court] is held, shall assemble to hear all complaints touching any wrongs and injuries inflicted on any persons by sheriffs, bailiffs, or any other men . . ." A council of twenty-four, twelve chosen by the king and twelve chosen by the barons, would oversee appointments to important offices, administration of the counties, and the management of royal castles. Parliament would meet three times per year to oversee the activities of the council. In 1259, Simon and his allies developed the Provisions of Westminster, which further refined the Provisions of Oxford, introducing inheritance and taxation reforms intended to prevent arbitrary measures by royal officials, expanding on similar clauses in Magna Carta.

The de Montfort faction developed the Provisions of Oxford and Westminster from existing precedents. By Henry III's reign, the councils of senior barons and clergymen summoned to advise successive English kings had become known as parliaments (after the French word *parlement*) for judicial bodies that served as courts of appeal. Simon aspired to expand the political class involved in decision making from the barons and bishops to include county knights and even burgesses from the towns, beginning the expansion of Magna Carta's rights from the elites to other social groups. This assembly became known as "the Commons," a term that survives to the present day. The unprecedented scope of Simon's reforms alarmed a number of his allies among the nobility and his faction began to splinter.

Henry appeared to accept both sets of provisions but, like John, he did not have any intention of accepting lasting limits on his power. Henry's eventual rejection of the provisions provided the impetus for a Second Barons' War. Simon achieved a significant victory at the Battle of Lewes on May 14, 1264, defeating the king's forces and taking Henry and his heir, the future Edward I, prisoner. The war turned against Simon in 1265 when Edward, a formidable soldier, escaped from his custody. Edward defeated de Montfort at the Battle of Evesham on August 4, 1265. Simon and his eldest son died on the battlefield. Without his leadership, the already divided opposition to Henry III's policies dissipated and the Second Barons' War came to an end in 1267.

Nineteenth-century artist's rendering of Simon de Montfort's death at the Battle of Evesham in 1265.

In victory, Henry and Edward rejected the Provisions of Oxford. Simon's death, however, was not in vain; his reforms had a lasting impact on the policies of both kings. Henry continued to summon the Commons to Parliament after the war in an attempt to reconcile himself with the nobility who did not support his military campaigns on the continent without being permitted a voice in government. The de Montfort parliament of January 1265 set precedents for a parliamentary system of representative government that included voices from various social classes. The precedents set by Montfort are still followed in modern times.

Part 3

The Decline and Revival of Magna Carta

Magna Carta addressed the breakdown of the relationship between King John and his barons in 1215. The key principles of the charter, however, including the right to due process, equality before the law, and judgment by peers, transcended the thirteenth century and inspired centuries of legislative and political reform. Monarchs throughout the late Middle Ages swore to uphold the principles of Magna Carta. The charter fell into a period of obscurity in the sixteenth century when strong monarchs enjoyed popular support, then experienced a revival in the early seventeenth century due to the writings of Sir Edward Coke, a renowned jurist whose career spanned the reigns of three English monarchs. Coke authored the 1628 Petition of Right that attempted to constrain the arbitrary rule of Charles I prior to the outbreak of the English Civil Wars, and his *Institutes of the Lawes of England* became the legal texts studied throughout the English-speaking world. Coke's view that "Magna Charta is such a fellow that he will have no sovereign"[10] shaped the political and legal history of the Western world, including the American Revolution, the French Revolution, and Canada's Confederation.

THE SPREAD OF MAGNA CARTA'S IDEALS FROM BARONS TO COMMONERS

In 1215, the strict social hierarchy of the thirteenth century limited the popular impact of Magna Carta. The majority of the principles in the charter addressed the concerns of landed barons and knights with specific clauses addressing the needs of the church, urban merchants, and the more general "free man," the term the charter used to describe all who were not bound by serfdom. The breakdown of the feudal system and the end of serfdom in the centuries following Magna Carta expanded the numbers of free peasantry and labourers until the charter applied to everyone officially. The rights intended for the landed nobility became universal in late medieval England.

The most recent copies of Magna Carta that are engrossed with a king's seal date from the reign of John's grandson, Edward I (r. 1272–1307). In contrast to his

King Edward III proclaiming Magna Carta.

queen, our manors, fair to hold." In these circumstances, Magna Carta was as relevant as it had been in 1215.

In contrast to Henry III and John, Edward was willing to work with his subjects to achieve his military and financial aims instead of dismissing their concerns. As heir to the throne, Edward had opposed Simon de Montfort, whose Provisions of Oxford called for regular parliaments, but his reign was marked by regular sessions of Parliament, where the king addressed the concerns of his subjects in exchange for authorization for new taxes to fund his military campaigns. Edward's 1295 Model Parliament had a broad composition similar to the 1265 de Montfort parliament, including knights and townspeople as well as barons and senior clergy. The 1295 Parliament served as a model for future parliaments in terms of its composition and purpose in presenting grievances to the monarch. Magna Carta served as the benchmark for the rights expected by the representatives in Parliament. For example, in 1300 the barons in Parliament agreed that "when we have secure possession of our forests and of our liberties, often promised to us, then we will willingly give a twentieth, so that the folly of the Scots may be dealt with." Parliament acted as the guarantor of the charter. Edward swore to uphold Magna Carta that same year and affixed his seal to a new revision of the charter. Edward's reign saw Magna Carta accepted as binding legislation for future monarchs. The clauses that remain on the statute books in the United Kingdom today from Magna Carta and Charter of the Forest date from the 1297 version of these charters issued by Edward I.

The reign of Edward I's grandson, Edward III (r. 1327–1377), saw the expansion of Magna Carta's

predecessors, Edward did not have any rivals to the throne and his succession was uncontested, even though he was on crusade at the time of his father's death. Edward had proven his abilities as a commander during the Second Barons' War and spent much of his reign at war with Wales and Scotland, earning the nickname, the Hammer of the Scots. Like John's attempts to recover his French domains, the conquest of Wales and invasion of Scotland required additional taxation. Edward and his queen had a reputation for personal acquisitiveness. According to a popular rhyme from Edward's reign, "The king would like to get our gold; the

King Edward I and his queen, Eleanor of Castile. Although both Edward and Eleanor had a reputation for acquisitiveness, Edward reissued Magna Carta and expressed a willingness to work with his barons.

The bubonic plague or Black Death arrived in England in 1348, resulting in the deaths of between one-third and one-half of England's inhabitants. The labour shortages created by the falling population contributed to the collapse of the feudal system. Edward III attempted to introduce measures that would protect the interests of the landed nobility. In 1351, the Statute of Labourers enacted a maximum wage, forbade workers from travelling to seek better working conditions, and imposed penalties for vagrancy. This statute led to peasant revolts, most famously the revolt faced by Edward III's grandson, Richard II, in 1381. In the long term, the statute would prove impossible to enforce. Magna Carta had been written to address the grievances of the elites, but during the period of social and economic change that followed the Black Death, the peasantry presented their own demands for guaranteed rights and freedoms.

The legal interpretation of Magna Carta changed in Edward III's reign to reflect the breakdown of the feudal system. A series of laws enacted between 1331 and 1369 and known as the Six Statutes changed the language used in the thirteenth-century versions of the charter, including people of all social hierarchies and making explicit reference to due process and trial by a jury of "good and lawful people of the same neighbourhood where such deeds be done." The statute passed in 1354 declared, "No man of whatever Estate or Condition that he be, shall be put out of Land or Tenement, nor taken nor imprisoned, nor disinherited, nor put to Death, without being brought in Answer by due Process of the Law," replacing Magna Carta's reference to "no free man" with "no man." By the fifteenth century, inclusion of women in this interpretation was

provisions to people of all social backgrounds. Edward III reigned during a period of profound social and demographic change that upset the social hierarchies taken for granted by his predecessors. The period of mostly warm temperatures that had prevailed during John's reign had come to an end. Increased harvests associated with a warmer climate had fed a growing population in John's reign and had created popular pressure for common stewardship of forest land. As the climate grew colder, harvests failed. The Great Famine of 1315–17 brought an end to the steady population growth that England had experienced since 1066.

King Edward III in the Robes of the Order of the Garter, which he founded.

in county courts to ensure that everyone was familiar with the charter, and late medieval litigants often cited the document in defence of their claims. Illuminated manuscripts depicted successive medieval monarchs consulting the charter and dispensing the law. The development of the rights codified in Magna Carta through the Six Statutes would have a profound impact on modern interpretations of the charter. Future legal scholars would consult the wording of the statutes rather than the original text from the reigns of John, Henry III, and Edward I to determine Magna Carta's significance in the modern world.

THE DECLINE OF MAGNA CARTA

The development of the printing press by Johannes Gutenberg around 1450 should have been an opportunity for increased dissemination of Magna Carta to an even wider audience. Gutenberg's innovations allowed for comparatively rapid production of printed matter, which gradually replaced the laborious process of copying documents by hand. Instead, Magna Carta experienced a period of obscurity that lasted from the mid-1400s until the early 1600s, becoming a text consulted by legal scholars alone instead of inspiring the general public. The Wars of the Roses (a series of dynastic wars fought between 1455 and 1485), the religious strife that accompanied the development of the Church of England in the 1530s, and the threat of foreign invasion during Elizabeth I's reign (1558–1603) appeared to demonstrate the need for strong monarchs who could act decisively without consulting their

made explicit as "ladies of great estate" received the right to judgment from men of their social class.

The reign of Edward III also saw Magna Carta treated as a cornerstone of the justice system that could not be superseded by future pieces of legislation. The 1368 statute declared, "If any Statute be made to the contrary, that shall be holden for none." The terms of Magna Carta were read aloud regularly

A nineteenth-century image of Act IV, Scene I, of Shakespeare's *King John*. In this scene, John's young nephew, Arthur of Brittany, pleads with his jailor, Hubert, to refuse the order from the King to put out his eyes. There is no mention of Magna Carta in Shakespeare's *King John*.

monarch to publicly swear to uphold the provisions of Magna Carta. Henry's reign also saw the introduction of formal legislation defining who had the right to vote, in place of the patchwork of customs concerning voter eligibility that existed in different regions in England. In 1430, the franchise was restricted to "forty-shilling freeholders," men who possessed property that generated an income of at least forty shillings per year. These requirements for voters remained unchanged until the Great Reform Bill of 1832 increased the franchise to a fifth of the adult male population.

Despite his intention to uphold Magna Carta, Henry VI was unable to govern effectively; historians speculate that he suffered from intermittent periods of a mental illness that may have been catatonic schizophrenia. Having only lately emerged from its prolonged and debilitating war against France (the Hundred Years War, 1337–1453), England found itself plunged into conflict between the Lancaster and York branches of the reigning Plantagenet dynasty; under the circumstances, strong central leadership appeared to be more desirable than rule based on consensus. Two of Henry VI's immediate successors, the Yorkist kings Edward IV and Richard III, claimed the throne through warfare and usurpation respectively rather than orderly succession, which disrupted continuity with the legislative reforms of past monarchs.

When the first Tudor king Henry VII (r. 1485–1509) defeated Richard III at the Battle of Bosworth Field in 1485, he claimed the throne by right of conquest. This approach differed from that of William the Conqueror in 1066, who claimed to be Edward the Confessor's lawful successor and therefore inherited Anglo-Saxon laws

subjects. The Yorkist and Tudor monarchs paid little attention to Magna Carta and dismissed the claims of those who attempted to invoke the charter. Magna Carta had largely drifted out of the popular consciousness by the death of Queen Elizabeth I in 1603.

Henry VI (r. 1422–1461 and 1470–1471) was the last monarch from the House of Lancaster and the last and customs. Having united the Houses of Lancaster and York through his marriage to Edward IV's eldest daughter, Elizabeth of York, Henry VII emphasized strong central leadership and focused his efforts on increasing the revenues of the crown. Henry VII imposed heavy fines on the nobility and established the Council Learned in the Law, which asserted existing royal prerogatives and created new ones without regard for existing laws and precedents. In this environment of increased royal authority, Magna Carta was a comparatively obscure document considered to be of interest to lawyers alone rather than the general public. The first printed edition of the Great Charter, published in 1508, was a Latin and French volume by Richard Pynson that was part of a compilation of *antiqua statuta* (ancient statutes) for legal reference.

There was potential for a rebirth of Magna Carta during the reign of Henry VII's son, Henry VIII (r. 1509–1547). Henry VIII was well educated and interested in the law. Throughout his reign, he applied a veneer of due process to even his most arbitrary actions. For example, the king's second wife, Anne Boleyn, and fifth wife, Catherine Howard, both received show trials convicting them of treason and adultery before their beheadings in 1536 and 1542 respectively. In contrast, Henry VIII's grandfather, Edward IV, reputedly ordered the drowning of his rebellious brother, George, in a barrel of malmsey wine without allowing him to contest the charge of treason.

Henry's controversial break with the papacy and establishment of the Church of England in the 1530s made the opening clause of Magna Carta, guaranteeing the freedom of the English church relevant to opponents of his religious policies. Both Henry's chancellor, Thomas

More, and the leader of the Pilgrimage of Grace rebellion of 1536, Robert Aske, cited Magna Carta to support their objections to the king's supremacy over the Church of England. Their appeals to the charter were unsuccessful. Henry VIII rejected any interpretation of the law that limited his power over either the church or the state. Both More and Aske were convicted of treason and executed in the mid-1530s.

The absence of any mention of Magna Carta in William Shakespeare's play, *The Life and Death of King John*, which was written in the 1590s, demonstrates the disappearance of the charter from popular consciousness in the sixteenth century. For Shakespeare, John's villainy was tempered by his willingness to confront the papacy in the manner of Henry VIII. Shakespeare and his audience would have had little sympathy for the rebel barons because they threatened England's independence by inviting a French invasion. In the play, John says to a cardinal:

> Tell [the pope] this tale; and from the mouth of England
> Add thus much more, that no Italian priest
> Shall tithe or toll in our dominions;
> But as we, under heaven, are supreme head,
> So under Him that great supremacy . . .

This language reflected sixteenth-century Protestant attitudes toward Catholicism rather than John's conflict with the papacy over the appointment of the archbishop of Canterbury in the early thirteenth century. To the Protestant subjects of Queen Elizabeth I (r. 1558–1603) in Shakespeare's audience, John appeared to be a

MAGNA CARTA AND ROYAL ABDICATION

Charles I is only the most famous example of an English monarch losing his throne because he ignored the rights and customs of his subjects. Opponents of Edward II (r. 1307–1327) and Richard II (r. 1377–1399) invoked Magna Carta to justify rebellion against a reigning monarch. In the Provisions of Oxford (1258), Simon de Montfort called for baronial councils to supervise the royal household. Kings who followed in Henry III's (r. 1216–1272) footsteps by upholding the rights of a few favourites instead of dispensing justice equally found themselves removed from office and replaced by relatives willing to uphold existing laws and customs. Edward II lavished wealth, titles, and land on Piers Gaveston and Hugh Despenser without regard for the interests of his fellow barons or the church. The nobility and clergy elected eight earls, seven bishops, and six untitled barons to draft the Ordinances of 1311, which required all clauses of Magna Carta to be upheld by the king. Edward II refused to accept limits on his power. Edward's discontented barons supported a coup by his queen, Isabella of France, who forced his abdication in 1327 with the assistance of foreign mercenaries engaged during an extended stay in Europe and ruled as regent on behalf of their teenage son, Edward III. Despenser was apprehended and executed by the queen's forces, and Edward II was quietly murdered in prison a few months after his abdication. In the case of Richard II, he had refused to allow his exiled cousin, Henry of Bolingbroke, to automatically come into his inheritance upon the death of his father, the immensely rich and powerful John of Gaunt, in 1399, thereby disinheriting a rival and violating the terms

Nineteenth-century engraving of King Henry IV, who forced the abdication of his cousin, Richard II, in 1399.

of Magna Carta. Henry invaded England, ostensibly to claim his rightful inheritance but more likely to dispatch the unpopular Richard. The king abdicated and Bolingbroke succeeded him as Henry IV that same year. Both Edward and Richard died under mysterious circumstances, ensuring that they would not become political rivals to their successors.

patriot and defender of an independent English church against papal interference.

Elizabethan Protestants believed that a strong monarch was necessary to defend England from external threats from the papacy or continental Roman Catholic kingdoms such as France and Spain. Elizabeth I encouraged her subjects to revere her as the embodiment of the English state. While Catholics traditionally displayed images of saints in their homes, Protestants kept images of the monarch. Odes to Elizabeth I described her in explicitly religious terms as a Protestant Deborah, the only female judge in the Old Testament, or Gloriana, the heroine of Edmund Spenser's epic poem *The Faerie Queen*, whose knights challenged Catholic adversaries. After the defeat of the Spanish Armada in 1588, a portrait of Elizabeth I emphasized her uncontested power with her hand encircling a small globe. The concerns of John's barons seemed remote to Elizabeth I's subjects. Magna Carta had passed into obscurity only to be rediscovered in the reign of Elizabeth's successor, James I.

SIR EDWARD COKE AND THE REBIRTH OF MAGNA CARTA

The revival of Magna Carta in the early seventeenth century arose from the writing and commentary of Sir Edward Coke (1552–1634). Modern perceptions of the charter's lasting significance reflect Coke's interpretations rather than the intentions of the rebel barons in 1215. Monarchs from the Scottish Stuart dynasty, who reigned in England from 1603 to 1714, had a broad range of political philosophies from monarchy by divine

Sir Edward Coke, a jurist whose career spanned the reigns of three monarchs, Elizabeth I, James I, and Charles I. Coke's writings contributed to the revival of Magna Carta in the popular imagination.

right during the reigns of James I and Charles I to constitutional monarchy during the reigns of William III and Mary II, and Anne. Coke's ideas spread with the expansion of the British Empire over the course of the seventeenth and eighteenth centuries. His views achieved widespread global influence, informing the political and legal institutions of the English-speaking world.

Over the course of his long career, Coke wrote thirteen volumes of law reports and the four-volume *Institutes of the Lawes of England*, which became a standard legal text throughout the English-speaking world. His writings, connections, and success as a lawyer for the King's Bench and the powerful dukes of Norfolk resulted in his rise to prominence over the course of Elizabeth I's reign. Coke became a member of Parliament, speaker of the House of Commons, and attorney general for England and Wales. Coke's stature enabled his views on Magna Carta to circulate to a wide audience of influential people, rescuing the charter from a century of relative obscurity.

For information about King John, his rebel barons, and Magna Carta, Coke and his fellow jurists drew upon the text of the 1297 version and Raphael Holinshed's *Chronicles of England, Scotland, and Ireland*, first published in 1577. The Holinshed book also served as source material for Shakespeare's historical plays. While Shakespeare omitted any reference to Magna Carta, early seventeenth-century jurists were drawn to Holinshed's description of John reluctantly affixing his seal to the charter. Holinshed wrote, "Finally, when the king, measuring his own strength with the barons, perceived that he was not able to resist them, he consented to subscribe and seal to such articles concerning the liberties demanded, in form for the most part as is contained in the two charters Magna Carta, and Carta de Foresta [the Charter of the Forest]."

Holinshed's chronicles provided the crucial link between John and Magna Carta. The later versions issued by Henry III and Edward I had confused the origin of the charter by the seventeenth century, fuelling the misconception that Magna Carta's clauses dated from a later reign. Coke's contemporary, John Cowell, wrote in *The Interpreter*, a dictionary of legal definitions, that Magna Carta was "a charter containing a number of laws ordained in the ninth year of Henry the third, and confirmed by Edward the first." Cowell assumed that John had accepted a precursor of Magna Carta rather than the charter itself, writing, "I reade in Holinshed that King John, to appease his Barons, yielded to laws or articles of government much like to this Great Charter, but we nowe have no [more ancient] written lawe than this." The misconceptions in the legal community regarding the origins of Magna Carta demonstrated how obscure the charter had become during the reigns of the Tudor monarchs.

Through his study of the historical context surrounding Magna Carta, Coke concluded that the charter codified English laws and customs that predated the Norman Conquest of 1066 and was therefore England's "ancient constitution." According to Coke, "It is called Magna Charta, not that it is great in quantity, but in respect of the great importance and weightiness of the matter." Coke's views may not have exactly matched the intentions of the rebel barons in 1215, but his interpretation spoke to the political circumstances of seventeenth-century England where jurists were in conflict with the new Stuart dynasty, which favoured absolute monarchy over the established constitutional tradition.

As chief justice of the Common Pleas from 1606 to 1613, Coke employed his interpretation of Magna Carta to affirm that not even the king was above the law. This stance was contrary to the views of King James I (r. 1603–1625), who succeeded to the throne upon the death of Elizabeth I. James was drawn to continental European ideas of divine right monarchy and viewed himself as an intellectual and legal expert.

Coke and James debated whether sovereignty arose from constitutional traditions or divine right in 1608. Coke later wrote that he had said to the king that "the law was a golden metwand [an obsolete form of measuring wand] and measure to try the causes of the subjects; and which protected his majesty in safety and peace; with which the king was greatly offended, and said, that then he should be under the law, which was treason to affirm." During the reign of Henry VIII, a direct challenge to the king's ability to rule with impunity would have ended Coke's legal career and probably his life. James, however, enjoyed intellectual debate and had a different approach to subjects with dissenting opinions. The king transferred Coke from the Common Pleas to chief justice of the King's Bench in 1613, where the jurist's legal acumen would directly serve the sovereign's interests. Despite this compromise, Coke eventually exhausted even James's patience with his "exorbitant and extravagant opinions." The king imprisoned Coke in the Tower of London for seven months in 1621, but the jurist was released and able to resume his legal career.

Coke had the greatest impact on the rebirth of Magna Carta in the early seventeenth century, but he was not the only one to remind the public of the rights enshrined in the charter at this time. According to Sir Henry Spellman, a member of Parliament and collector of medieval documents, Magna Carta was "the most majestic and a sacrosanct anchor to English liberties." The attorney Frances Ashley, another contemporary of Coke's, argued in 1616 that Magna Carta contained "the sum and substance" of the Anglo-Saxon law code that predated the Norman Conquest of 1066. Coke's writings informed a wider rediscovery of Magna Carta by England's political elites during the early seventeenth century.

Coke's belief that "Magna Charta is such a fellow that he will have no sovereign" and that not even the monarch was above the law of the land transformed the charter from an obscure legal document to the cornerstone of modern justice, law, and human rights. The rebirth of Magna Carta had direct political consequences in England as Coke's interpretation of the Charter informed limits on the monarch's power through the Petition of Right in 1628 and the eventual outbreak of the English Civil Wars in 1642.

THE PETITION OF RIGHT IN 1628

The culmination of Coke's long legal career was his role in enshrining Magna Carta's provisions in the Petition of Right in 1628. James I's son, Charles I (r. 1625–1649), was far less tolerant of opposing viewpoints than his father. Like James, Charles considered himself king by divine right. While James usually relished intellectual debate, Charles had little interest in discussing his prerogatives with his subjects. Charles made efforts to censor Coke's writings, but the jurist's commentaries on Magna Carta continued to be topical because the new king soon found himself in conflict with Parliament.

In 1626, Charles dissolved Parliament because of its opposition to the influence of his closest friend, George Villiers, Duke of Buckingham, over military and

﹅ The Petition of Right informed future English legislation such as the 1689 Bill of Rights that established the modern constitutional monarchy. This engraving depicts the coronation of Charles I's grandchildren, William III and Mary II, after they accepted the Bill of Rights from Parliament.

Bust of Charles I on St. Margaret's Church, across from the Houses of Parliament. Charles I's refusal to uphold the Petition of Right contributed to the outbreak of the English Civil Wars.

political matters. Without Parliament to approve taxation, Charles imposed a forced loan on his subjects, calling upon them to "lovingly, freely and voluntarily" contribute to his expenses. Seventy-six members of the landed gentry and the Earl of Lincoln were imprisoned for their refusal to pay, though Charles avoided pressing formal changes to prevent the courts from ruling on the legality of forced loans imposed by the Crown. Counsel on behalf of five of the imprisoned knights, including Thomas Darnel, issued legal writs of habeas corpus to receive bail. When the case was heard by the King's Bench in November 1627, the defence cited the clause of Magna Carta that forbade imprisonment without due process. Other rights were attributed to Magna Carta that were not part of the thirteenth-century versions of

the charter, including freedom from taxation without parliamentary consent. The prosecution won the Five Knight's Case, or Darnel's Case, because there were also past precedents for monarchs imprisoning their subjects without due process. The ruling was extremely controversial because these past instances had involved threats to the security of the kingdom rather than refusal to provide an arbitrarily imposed loan to the monarch.

Charles I recalled Parliament in 1628, expecting the members to approve new taxes to finance ongoing hostilities with France. Instead, the king faced a debate over the nature of his sovereignty in response to his treatment of the imprisoned knights. Parliament decided to present the king with a seventeenth-century version of Magna Carta that would place his powers within the rule of law. Coke chaired the committee that authored this document, the Petition of Right, and his interpretation of the significance of Magna Carta to English law shaped the text. The Petition of Right also reflected the influence of the Six Statutes passed during the reign of Edward III, which expanded the scope of Magna Carta's provisions.

The third clause of the Petition of Right quoted Magna Carta directly, stating, "By the statute called 'The Great Charter of the Liberties of England,' it is declared and enacted, that no freeman may be taken or imprisoned or be disseized of his freehold or liberties, or his free customs, or be outlawed or exiled, or in any manner destroyed, but by the lawful judgment of his peers, or by the law of the land."

Following the invocation of Magna Carta as a charter that summarized the "Liberties of England," the Petition of Right made explicit reference to the statute from Edward III's reign that extended these rights to

THE EVOLUTION OF THE CHARTER OF THE FOREST IN THE SIXTEENTH AND SEVENTEENTH CENTURIES

Just as interpretations of Magna Carta varied over the centuries, the significance of the Charter of the Forest also changed according to political circumstances. John and his predecessors zealously protected their exclusive right to hunt large game in the forests. For the Tudor monarchs of the sixteenth century, however, the key resource on forest land was the timber necessary to build ships. Henry VIII romanticized the Hundred Years War (1337–1453) and made a number of attempts to reclaim former English territories in France. Elizabeth I faced a Spanish Armada in 1588. War with France then Spain required timber for the building of new ships. Henry VIII placed the royal forests under the Court of Augmentations, the same judicial body in charge of exacting revenue from the dissolution of the monasteries and convents during the English Reformation of the 1530s. When James I succeeded to the throne in 1603, he made inquiries regarding the extent of cleared land and private property within royal forests. During Charles I's rule without Parliament between 1629 and 1640, he treated the forests as a source of revenue in the manner of John, "disafforesting" lands for a fee, a process that exempted inhabitants from forest law, and selling undeveloped land for a profit. Charles I's arbitrary treatment of forest inhabitants prompted the Western Rising, a series of riots in Gillingham, Baydon, Dean, and Feckenham forests protesting the enclosure of common resources by the new owners of former royal forests. The riots continued during the English Civil Wars (1642–1651) and the Interregnum (1649–1660), demonstrating that forest residents continued to expect common stewardship of shared resources, in keeping with the provisions of the Charter of the Forest.

The execution of Charles I in 1649. Even Charles I expected to be judged by his peers.

people of all social backgrounds, stating, "And in the eight-and-twentieth year of the reign of King Edward III, it was declared and enacted by authority of Parliament, that no man, of what estate or condition that he be, should be put out of his land or tenements, nor taken, nor imprisoned, nor disinherited nor put to death without being brought to answer by due process of law."

The petition went on to explain how the king had violated these principles by imposing a forced loan then arresting those who refused to pay. Charles I resisted giving royal assent to the Petition of Right because of the limits it imposed on his powers, accusing the House of Commons of interfering with affairs of state that were not within its jurisdiction. Charles, following assurances from jurists that he would be able to maintain absolute authority in extraordinary circumstances, reluctantly accepted the Petition of Right in June 1628.

The Petition of Right ultimately failed to impose lasting limits on Charles I's rule. In 1629, the year after he reluctantly accepted this new legislation, the king prorogued Parliament and reigned without checks and balances for eleven years. Like John, Charles I was accused of arbitrary rule by his subjects. During his period of Personal Rule, he revived old medieval taxes without the consent of subjects. For example, he demanded "ship money" from coastal towns — a traditional feudal due intended to pay for the defence of these regions.

Without Parliament to provide oversight regarding the budget, there was rampant speculation that this tax revenue was being diverted to cover the king's personal expenses. One pamphlet accused the king of using ship money to support his infamous mother-in-law, Marie de Medici, stating, "Reasons why ship and conduct money ought to be had and also money [lent] by the City of London. Wherever the Queen mother has been there could be no peace, yet ship and conduct money must be had to keep her . . ." Charles I's rule without Parliament was perceived to be as arbitrary as that of John before the drafting of Magna Carta.

In the absence of Parliament, Charles I appeared to be acting on the advice of unpopular advisers, including his Roman Catholic French queen, Henrietta Maria, and William Laud, the archbishop of Canterbury. Laud was particularly unpopular with British Protestants who were not part of the Church of England, such as Puritans and Presbyterian Scots, because he attempted to impose a High Church Anglican liturgy on all of Charles I's subjects. These religious tensions led to the outbreak of the Bishops' War between England and Scotland in 1640. Charles I did not have the revenue necessary to continue hostilities against his Scottish subjects and therefore reluctantly recalled Parliament that same year.

THE ENGLISH CIVIL WARS AND THE INTERREGNUM

The Long Parliament, which sat from 1640 to 1648, refused to approve new taxes without reform enacted according to Coke's interpretation of Magna Carta. Coke had died in 1634, but Parliament issued instructions to his estate, stating, "This House doth desire, and hold it fit, that the heir of Sir Edward Cooke [*sic*] do publish in Print his Commentary upon Magna Carta, The Pleas of the Crown, and The Jurisdiction of Courts, according

Statue of Oliver Cromwell outside the Houses of Parliament. Oliver Cromwell was dismissive of Magna Carta and the Petition of Right.

to the intention of the said Sir Edward Cooke [*sic*]." The instructions demonstrate that Coke's commentary on Magna Carta, rather than the original documents from the thirteenth century, had become the standard version of the charter that informed the political process in the mid-seventeenth century.

Relations between Charles and Parliament broke down entirely by January 1642, when the king attempted to arrest five members of the House of Commons personally. The five members had been warned of their impending arrest and fled. Their fellow members of Parliament refused to reveal their whereabouts, considering the king's presence in the chamber inappropriate. To this day, the doors to the House of Commons are slammed in the face of the Gentleman Usher of the Black Rod each year at the State Opening of Parliament to demonstrate that neither monarchs nor representatives may enter the chamber without the permission of the House.

In August 1642, Charles I raised the royal standard at Nottingham, beginning the English Civil Wars between king and Parliament. Charles's forces, known as Cavaliers, were united by their loyalty to the king. Supporters of Parliament, known as Roundheads, were divided in their intentions. As the English Civil Wars progressed, a growing number of Roundheads sought to abolish the monarchy, but during the early years of the conflict, the main goal was to ensure that the king governed according to the Petition of Right and dismissed unpopular advisers.

Magna Carta and Coke's commentaries on the charter were published numerous times during the conflict with titles such as "Briefe Collections out of Magna Charta: or the Knowne good old Lawes of England," which was printed in 1643. The defeat of the royalist forces at the Battle of Naseby in 1645, coupled with Charles's unwillingness to compromise his prerogatives or keep his promises to his subjects contributed to his eventual trial for treason against his people in January 1649.

Despite having rejected constraints on his rule that arose from Magna Carta, Charles I invoked a key passage from the charter at his trial. The king refused to recognize the legality of the proceedings because he would not be receiving judgment from his peers. Charles argued that only other monarchs were entitled to judge his actions rather than the members of Parliament. Even a monarch who had claimed to rule by divine right expected to be judged by his peers as guaranteed by Magna Carta. Despite Charles's refusal to recognize the legitimacy of the trial or enter a plea, he was convicted of high treason in the name of the people of England and beheaded in front of Whitehall Palace on January 30, 1649.

The Protectorate that governed England during the interregnum between the execution of Charles I in 1649 and the restoration of his son, Charles II, in 1660, was not a democracy. Oliver Cromwell governed as Lord Protector from 1653 to 1658 and bequeathed this position to his eldest surviving son, Richard, in the manner of a monarch. Cromwell was the third member of Parliament to sign Charles I's death warrant, but his actions as Lord Protector demonstrated that he shared the king's intolerance for dissent and contempt for Magna Carta. In 1655, Cromwell declared to the judiciary that "their Magna Farta should not

control his actions which he knew were for the safety of the commonwealth." A late-seventeenth-century author claimed that Cromwell had even less use for the Petition of Right, calling it "The Petition of Shite." Cromwell, however, had the support of the New Model Army and was able to hold together disparate factions within Parliament. His son, Richard, however, did not have military experience and was unable to command the same support. In 1660, Parliament invited Charles I's eldest son back to England from exile in Europe to reign as Charles II.

THE BILL OF RIGHTS AND THE EMERGENCE OF CONSTITUTIONAL MONARCHY

The Restoration of the English monarchy in 1660 did not result in a return to the arbitrary rule that characterized the reign of Charles I. Instead, Charles II and his successors presided over the development of a constitutional monarchy, which remains the system of government in the United Kingdom, Canada, and fourteen other Commonwealth realms. The key document in the establishment of the constitutional monarchy — the 1689 Bill of Rights accepted by William III and Mary II — reflected the influence on English law of the revival of Magna Carta as interpreted by Coke in the Petition of Right.

Charles II recognized the importance of working with Parliament after the upheaval of the English Civil Wars and even saw the advantages of distancing himself from day-to-day government business. One of the king's closest friends, John Wilmot, second Earl of

Nineteenth-century engraving of King William III. William III and his wife, Mary II, were England's first constitutional monarchs.

Rochester, wrote, "We have a pretty witty king, / Whose word no man relies on, / He never said a foolish thing, / And never did a wise one." When Charles was told of the verse, he quipped, "That's true, for my words are my own, but my actions are those of my ministers." In contrast, Charles's younger brother and successor, the Roman Catholic James II, lost the support of his Protestant subjects as he removed ministers from office who disagreed with his policies. In 1688, Parliament invited James II's Protestant son-in-law, William of Orange, to invade England from his native Holland and claim the throne, an event that became known as the Glorious Revolution. William and his wife, Mary, were acclaimed joint monarchs after Parliament judged that James II had "abdicated the government" and left the throne "vacant" by fleeing William's invading force.

The Glorious Revolution had a more lasting impact than previous royal abdications because William III and Mary II became England's first constitutional monarchs, accepting permanent limits on their power and the powers of their successors by ratifying the Bill of Rights in 1689. The bill listed James II's various transgressions, including ". . . assuming and exercising a power of dispensing with and suspending of laws, and the execution of laws, without consent of Parliament" and "prosecutions in the court of King's bench, for matters and causes cognizable only in Parliament; and by divers other arbitrary and illegal courses."

William and Mary were asked to affirm numerous limits on their power, including "That the pretended power of suspending of laws, or the execution of laws, by regal authority, without consent of Parliament, is illegal . . . That the pretended power of dispensing with laws, or the executions of laws, by regal authority, as it hath been assumed and exercised of late, is illegal." In contrast to John and Charles I who quickly repudiated the Magna Carta and Petition of Right respectively, William and Mary's successors continued to observe the Bill of Rights, allowing the development of constitutional monarchy over the course of subsequent centuries.

The late seventeenth century also saw the earliest attempts to place Magna Carta in its proper historical context after centuries of interpretations based on the political circumstances faced by successive jurists. Opponents of the growing powers of Parliament emphasized that Magna Carta was an agreement between John and his barons rather than a universal charter of liberties. In 1684, in his *Introduction to the Old English Liberties*, Robert Brady wrote, "Sir Edward Coke hath a fine fetch to play off the Great Charter and interpret it by his modern lawe." This historical interpretation attracted little interest, since as the development of the modern constitutional monarchy through the Petition of Right and Bill of Rights appeared to demonstrate a clear continuum of English monarchs accepting limits on their power imposed by their subjects.

The office of the prime minister as Head of Government emerged during the reign of King George I (r. 1714–1727). George was the first king of Great Britain from the German House of Hanover and he was unable to speak English fluently. The parliaments of England and Scotland had united in 1707 to form a single British government, and Britain's first prime minister, Robert Walpole, declared "Whatever are the Rights of Men in this Age, were their Rights in Every Age; For rights are independent of power." Walpole assumed power after the South Sea Bubble economic crisis of 1720 undermined the king's authority.

Walpole was a member of the Whig political party, which favoured the Commons over the monarchy, and supported the idea that Magna Carta both codified ancient rights and was a foundational document in the development of Common Law, which became known as part of the Whig interpretation of history. The division of powers between the monarch as Head of State and the prime minister as Head of Government continued in the eighteenth century. The monarch retained extensive influence over foreign policy until the end of Queen Victoria's reign (r. 1837–1901), but domestic affairs became the domain of the prime minister.

The seventeenth century saw the revival of Magna Carta as a popular cornerstone of political and legal rights, informing the creation of new documents that established a lasting constitutional monarchy that remained the system of government in the United Kingdom and Canada. Modern interpretations of Magna Carta are not informed by the intentions of thirteenth-century rebel barons but by seventeenth-century jurists — most notably, Sir Edward Coke through his leading role in the authorship of the Petition of Right. It was Coke's interpretation of Magna Carta that travelled outside England through his authorship of legal textbooks, influencing the outbreak of the American Revolution. Coke's commentaries also informed the spread of Magna Carta's ideals to other regions of the English-speaking world, including Canada.

Part 4

Magna Carta Abroad

Europe's age of exploration coincided with the rebirth of Magna Carta. As British settlers established colonies in North America, they took their political and legal institutions with them, including the ideals codified in Magna Carta. In British North America, the Royal Proclamation of 1763 established a special relationship between the Crown and the First Nations that exists in Canada to the present day. The colonial charters for the thirteen British colonies that eventually became the eastern seaboard of the United States of America were developed at the same time as Coke's commentaries on Magna Carta, and Coke himself authored the Virginia charter. Magna Carta shaped the political discourse that led to the American Revolution and Canada's Confederation. Magna Carta did not only spread across the Atlantic but to the rest of Europe as well. The Declaration of the Rights of Man and the Citizen that emerged from the French Revolution connects the Magna Carta to modern human rights documents, including the United Nations' Universal Declaration of Human Rights.

CANADA'S FIRST CONSTITUTIONAL DOCUMENT: THE ROYAL PROCLAMATION OF 1763

In 2013, Canada commemorated the 250th anniversary of the Royal Proclamation issued by King George III in 1763. The CBC described this historic charter as Canada's "Indian Magna Carta,"[11] referring to the document's significance in establishing the land rights of Canada's First Nations. There are numerous parallels between Magna Carta and the Royal Proclamation as an agreement regarding land ownership and legal rights between the monarch and his subjects. The Treaty of Paris, which ended the Seven Years' War or French and Indian War (1756–1763), was between Great Britain and France. The treaty ignored the concerns of the First Nations who fought in the conflict. The Iroquois Confederacy was a traditional ally of the British and expected to be recognized for its contributions to the conquest of French Canada during the conflict. The Royal Proclamation

King George III, who issued the Royal Proclamation in 1763.

of British citizens, including the rights guaranteed by Magna Carta as interpreted by the Petition of Right and Bill of Rights, stating, "all Persons Inhabiting in or resorting to our Said Colonies may confide in our Royal Protection for the Enjoyment of the Benefit of the Laws of our Realm of England."

First Nations in the newly acquired colony of Quebec were placed under the protection of the Crown and guaranteed their land rights. The first part of the document focused on the new boundaries of British North America and the land grants to be provided for British military personnel according to rank. Following these provisions, the proclamation explained First Nations rights in language reminiscent of Magna Carta.

Magna Carta ordered the removal of foreign mercenaries from English territory, stating, "Immediately after concluding peace we will remove from the kingdom all alien knights, crossbowmen, sergeants and mercenary soldiers who have come with horses and arms to the hurt of the realm." The Royal Proclamation similarly ordered unauthorized settlers to remove themselves from Native land, stating, "We do further strictly enjoin and require all Persons whatever who have either wilfully or inadvertently seated themselves upon any Lands within the Countries above described, or upon any other Lands which, not having been ceded to or purchased by Us, are still reserved to the said Indians as aforesaid, forthwith to remove themselves from such Settlements." Land west of the Appalachian Mountains was declared Indian Territory, and European settlers and their descendants were forbidden to settle in this territory and make unauthorized land purchases. There was potential for the boundary to move westward in the

established a special relationship between the Crown and Canada's First Nations and set precedents concerning Native land rights that continue to the present day, serving as Canada's first constitutional document.

The Royal Proclamation promised all inhabitants of newly acquired British colonies the rights and liberties future, but the proclamation intended for land transfers to occur in an orderly manner, taking First Nations' interests into account in their role as allies of the British.

The Crown promised justice to Canada's First Nations in 1763 as subjects of the Crown. The proclamation observed that "great Frauds and Abuses have been committed in purchasing Lands of the Indians, to the great Prejudice of our Interests, and to the great Dissatisfaction of the said Indians" and therefore forbade private sales of Native land. Land transactions were to be concluded at public assemblies presided over by the governor or commander-in-chief of the colony, "to the end that the Indians may be convinced of our Justice and determined Resolution to remove all reasonable Cause of Discontent." Just as Magna Carta had declared an end to arbitrary rule, the Royal Proclamation attempted to end arbitrary treatment of First Nations land rights to ensure orderly land transfers in British North America and a continued alliance between British and Native leaders. In 1764, two thousand chiefs representing twenty-four First Nations ratified the Royal Proclamation in the first Treaty of Fort Niagara.

More than 250 years after its creation, the Royal Proclamation remains integral to the Canadian government's relationship with the First Nations of Canada. According to section 25 of the Canadian Charter of Rights and Freedoms, "The guarantee in this Charter of certain rights and freedoms shall not be construed as to abrogate or derogate from any aboriginal, treaty or other rights or freedoms that pertain to the aboriginal peoples of Canada including (a) any rights or freedoms that have been recognized by the Royal Proclamation of October 7, 1763; and (b) any rights or freedoms that now exist by way of land claims agreements or may be

Governor William Hobson and the Maori chiefs signing the Treaty of Waitangi in New Zealand in 1840.

so acquired." Idle No More, a Canadian First Nations grassroots protest movement, described the proclamation as "the first document in which an imperial nation recognized indigenous sovereignty and their right to self-determination" and issued a call to action to coincide with the 250th anniversary of the document.[12]

The Royal Proclamation served as a precedent for future accords between the British and indigenous peoples throughout the world. The modern state of New Zealand exists because of the 1840 Treaty of Waitangi between Great Britain and the Maori people. The Maori ceded governance of their lands to Britain in exchange for protection by the Crown. Like the Royal Proclamation, the Treaty of Waitangi has been interpreted as a guarantee of autonomy and land rights for indigenous peoples. In 1975, New Zealand established the Waitangi Tribunal to investigate the treatment of the Maori people by the Crown since 1840, identifying breaches of the treaty and suggesting compensation for affected parties.

In 1763, the immediate impact of the Royal Proclamation was to allow most British troops to depart from the newly acquired regions of British North America after the end of hostilities with France, having reached an accord with the Native population. In 1774, the British North America (Quebec) Act guaranteed the practice of the Roman Catholic faith and use of French civil law in what is now Quebec, placing the rights of French Canadians under the protection of the Crown as well. While the Royal Proclamation and Quebec Act created the conditions for peace in what is now Canada, inhabitants of the thirteen colonies, now the eastern United States, were angered by these documents because they restricted settlement west of the Appalachian Mountains and gave special protection to the rights of French Canadians, who had been the enemy during the French and Indians War.

The withdrawal of British troops also increased scrutiny of taxation of the colonists without representation in Britain's Parliament, since these funds were no longer being spent on the defence of the colonies from the French. A growing number of colonists came to believe that Britain was violating the rights guaranteed to them by Magna Carta, conditions that led to the outbreak of the American Revolution.

THE AMERICAN REVOLUTION

The American colonists at the time of the American Revolution (1775–1783) were familiar both with Magna Carta as interpreted by Coke and the Petition of Right; they fully expected Great Britain to respect their rights according to the terms of the charter. Coke wrote his *Institutes of the Lawes of England* at a time when Britain was establishing the thirteen colonies, and they became the standard legal texts on both sides of the Atlantic. The first permanent British settlement in North America, Jamestown, was founded in 1607. Although Coke never visited the colony, he was closely involved in its development, contributing his legal expertise to the drafting of the Charter to the Virginia Company in 1606, which set precedents for subsequent colonial charters. This charter granted the colonists the same rights enjoyed by English people, stating that all inhabitants of Virginia, "shall HAVE and enjoy all Liberties, Franchises, and Immunities, within any of our other Dominions, to all Intents and Purposes, as if they had been abiding and born, within this our Realm of England, or any other of our said Dominions." These liberties included the legal rights codified in Magna Carta.

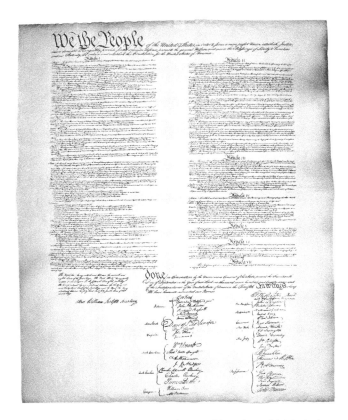

The Constitution of the United States of America, which includes the Bill of Rights, informed by Magna Carta and the Petition of Right.

A number of founding charters elsewhere in the colonies followed the template established by Virginia regarding the guarantee of the liberties enjoyed by the inhabitants of England, including Magna Carta. Charters drafted after 1628 reflected the influence of the Petition of Right. The first printed version of Magna Carta in the Americas was commissioned by William Penn, the founder of the state of Pennsylvania in 1687. With immigrants arriving in the thirteen colonies from outside Britain, Penn wanted to ensure that new colonists "that are strangers, in a great measure" reached "the true understanding of that inestimable Inheritance that every Free-born Subject of England is Heir unto by birthright, I mean that unparallel'd Priviledge of Liberty and Property." Knowledge of the rights codified in Magna Carta was considered necessary for all residents of the thirteen colonies, regardless of their background.

The 1689 Bill of Rights in England had less influence in the thirteen colonies because the establishment of the constitutional monarchy appeared to affirm Parliament's supremacy. The Bill of Rights granted parliament the ability to draft legislation that superseded previous charters of rights such as Magna Carta. While Great Britain maintained an unwritten constitution, the thirteen colonies treated Coke's commentaries on Magna Carta as inalienable rights that could not be altered by subsequent legislation. Laws that violated Coke's interpretation of Magna Carta were considered invalid. For example, when lawyer Silas Downer dedicated a "liberty tree" in Providence, Rhode Island, in 1768, he declared, "The great charter of liberties, commonly called Magna Carta, doth not give the privileges therein mentioned, nor doth our Charters, but must be considered only declaratory of our rights, and in affirmance of them." According to Downer, Magna Carta represented natural law and could not be superseded to justify new taxes or contrary legislation.

In the second half of the eighteenth century, lawyers and political figures in the thirteen colonies focused on the clauses of Magna Carta that codified freedom from arbitrary taxation and protection of private property as they faced a series of unpopular taxes imposed by the

British parliament. Britain imposed the Stamp Act in 1765, a direct tax that required all printed materials to be produced on English paper that bore an embossed revenue stamp. Since this tax raised the cost of legal documents, newspapers, and books, it attracted particular criticism from the colonists best educated in legal interpretations of Magna Carta.

The Massachusetts Assembly declared the Stamp Act "against the Magna Carta and the natural rights of Englishmen, and therefore, according to Lord Coke, null and void." The British parliament voted to repeal the unpopular Stamp Act in 1766; the decision, however, was accompanied by the Declaratory Act that affirmed Britain's right to legislate for the thirteen colonies. This new act was greeted by protests throughout the colonies, with protestors calling for "Magna Carta." The conflict between the political elites of Great Britain and the colonies regarding whether Parliament had the right to pass legislation that violated Coke's interpretation of Magna Carta contributed to the outbreak of the American Revolution.

The thirteen colonies that became the United States of America adopted the Declaration of Independence on July 4, 1776. The authors of this document were closely familiar with Magna Carta and Coke's commentaries. Future president Thomas Jefferson wrote to another future president, James Madison, praising Coke's work, stating, "A sounder Whig never wrote, nor of profounder learning in the orthodox doctrines of the British constitution, or in what were called English liberties." Americans observed the differences between British and American interpretations of Magna Carta. John Leland, a Baptist minister, wrote in 1794, "There

↖ Portrait bust of Thomas Jefferson who admired Coke's commentaries on Magna Carta.

is no constitution in Britain . . . although they consider the seventy-two articles of the Magna Charta as the basis of their government, yet from that basis they have never formed a constitution to describe the limits of each department of government. So precedents and parliamentary acts are all the constitution they have." The United States prevented future legislation from superseding Magna Carta by embedding the seventeenth-century interpretation of the document into their written Constitution.

THE HAITIAN REVOLUTION

When abolitionist Frederick Douglass opened the Haitian Pavilion at the 1893 World's Fair, he observed that a key difference between the American Revolution and the Haitian Revolution of 1804 was that the Americans had knowledge of Magna Carta. "Their ancestry," stated Douglas, "were the men who had defied the powers of royalty and wrested from an armed and reluctant king the grandest declaration of human rights ever given to the world . . .They belonged to the ruling race of this world and the sympathy of the world was with them. But far different was it with the men of Haiti. The world was all against them." Magna Carta may not have influenced the slaves who rebelled against their masters, but the French Revolution and the Declaration of the Rights of Man created the conditions that contributed to the success of the Haitian Revolution. Landed delegates to France's National Constituent Assembly from Saint-Domingue (the island's name prior to the revolution) debated racial discrimination according to the new rights enshrined in the declaration. Mixed-race landowners argued that white French immigrants were trying to create an "aristocracy of the skin" by attempting to limit their property rights on racial grounds. These conflicts among Saint-Domingue property owners provided an opportunity for the enslaved population to rebel against a divided ruling class. The National Assembly first decided to exempt France's Caribbean colonies from the terms of the declaration, but its successor, the National Convention, ultimately voted to abolish slavery in 1794. The decree was observed inconsistently in the French Caribbean, and in 1802 Napoleon Bonaparte legalized slavery once more. This attempt to re-establish slavery was unsuccessful in Saint-Domingue. The Republic of Haiti was proclaimed in 1804.

Eng.d by Augustus Robin. N.Y.

Fred.k Douglass.

The United States Bill of Rights, the first ten amendments of the Constitution of the United States of America.

The United States became a republic with the president assuming roles that were divided between the monarch and prime minister in Britain. The presidency was granted powers similar to that of the British monarch in the late eighteenth century such as the ability to declare war or make peace, issue pardons, and appoint ambassadors subject to the approval of Congress. The Petition of Right informs four of the first ten amendments to the United States Constitution, known as the Bill of Rights, thereby placing the legacy of Magna Carta directly within the framework of American law.

For example, the Fifth Amendment states:

No person shall be held to answer for a capital, or otherwise infamous crime, unless on a presentment or indictment of a Grand Jury . . . nor shall be compelled in any criminal case to be a witness against himself, nor be deprived of life, liberty, or property, without due process of law; nor shall private property be taken for public use, without just compensation.

This mirrors the third clause in the Petition of Right:

And whereas also by the statute called "The Great Charter of the Liberties of England," it is declared and enacted, that no freeman may be taken or imprisoned or be disseized of his freehold or liberties, or his free customs, or be outlawed or exiled, or in any manner destroyed, but by the lawful judgment of his peers, or by the law of the land.

It also draws on the fourth clause, which states, "that no man, of what estate or condition that he be, should be put out of his land or tenements, nor taken, nor imprisoned, nor disinherited nor put to death without being brought to answer by due process of law." Magna Carta, as interpreted by Coke in the Petition of Right, remains part of the American Constitution to the present day.

The role of Magna Carta in the American Revolution and the Constitution allowed the document to assume a totemic status in the American popular imagination. The image of King John accepting the Magna Carta from one of his barons is embossed on the doors of the

Supreme Court of the United States and a version of the charter from the reign of Edward I is on permanent display at the National Archives.

THE FRENCH REVOLUTION

The influence of Magna Carta on the 1789 *Déclaration des droits de l'homme et du citoyen* (Declaration of the Rights of Man and the Citizen), the key human rights document that emerged from the French Revolution, demonstrates that the charter's influence had expanded beyond the English-speaking world by the late eighteenth century. France had been defeated by Great Britain in the Seven Years' War, and the French king, Louis XVI (r. 1774–1791), viewed the American Revolution as an opportunity to weaken Britain's power around the world. The American Revolution proved to be the precursor to the French Revolution. Louis sent French troops to assist the American colonists, and they returned to France with ideas for reforming the state inspired by the American Declaration of Independence and the Constitution. Prominent American politicians and diplomats, including Benjamin Franklin and Thomas Jefferson, spent extended periods of time in France, sharing their views with French society.

The American Revolution also had a financial impact on the future of the French state. French military involvement in the conflict bankrupted Louis's regime. Like Charles I, Louis was obliged to summon a representative assembly to address his financial difficulties. In contrast to Great Britain, France did not have a consistent history of representative gov-

The storming of the Bastille, July 14, 1789, a key event of the French Revolution.

ernment. When Louis summoned the *États Généraux* (Estates General) in May 1789, it was the first time representatives of the clergy (the first estate), the nobility (the second estate), and common people (the third estate) had gathered to advise the king since 1614.

Like England's House of Commons in 1640, the Estates General expected political reform in exchange for alleviating the monarch's financial distress. The parallels between the situations of Charles I and Louis XVI were recognized during the French Revolution and debated in revolutionary pamphlets such as the 1793

King Louis XVI initially became a constitutional monarch during the French Revolution but was forced to abdicate in 1792 after attempting to flee Paris in 1791.

social estates. Louis XVI was obliged to accept limits on his powers, thus becoming a constitutional monarch, until his attempt to flee France in 1791 precipitated his arrest and trial in 1792 and execution in 1793.

In August 1789, the National Constituent Assembly issued The Declaration of the Rights of Man and the Citizen. Like the rebel barons of King John's reign, the deputies who drafted this document intended to affirm that no individual person, not even the monarch, was above the law. In contrast to Magna Carta, however, the deputies viewed the declaration as a statement of universal rights rather than a response to the political circumstances of the time alone. The French revolutionaries viewed themselves as part of a long political tradition of subjects holding their monarch to account and hoped that their principles would spread beyond France.

The Declaration of the Rights of Man included clauses reminiscent of Magna Carta, as interpreted by the Charter of the Forest, the Petition of Right, the Bill of Rights, and the Six Statutes. The declaration began, "Men are born and remain free and equal in rights. Social distinctions may be based only on common utility," reflecting how Magna Carta's provisions had been expanded to include everyone instead of only the landed nobility. Just as the Charter of the Forest called for common stewardship of shared resources, the declaration stated, "Liberty consists in the ability to do whatever does not harm another; hence the exercise of the natural rights of each man has no other limits than those which assure to other members of society the enjoyment of the same rights. These limits can only be determined by the law."

publication, "L'Angleterre Instruisant la France ou Tableau: Historique et Politique du Regne de Charles I et de Charles II."[12] The Estates General transformed into the *Assemblée nationale constituante* (National Constituent Assembly) in July 1789, representing the people as a whole instead of the three traditional

↘ Versailles Palace outside Paris. The palace was stormed in October 1789 and the royal family was moved to the Tuileries Palace in Paris.

The famous clause in Magna Carta that had been enshrined as the right to due process and freedom from arbitrary arrest appeared in the declaration as "No man may be indicted, arrested, or detained except in cases determined by law and according to the forms, which it has prescribed." In the event of an arrest and conviction, only "strictly and obviously necessary punishments may be established by the law." The ideals expressed in the declaration were not upheld over the course of the French Revolution. The National Convention, which held power in France from 1792 to 1795, instituted a Reign of Terror characterized by arbitrary arrest and thousands of executions by guillotine. The Civil Code established by Napoleon I in 1804 reversed numerous

87

↘ The Conciergerie in Paris became a prison during the Terror.

↘ Olympe de Gouges, author of the Declaration of the Rights of Woman and the Female Citizen.

new laws introduced during the early years of the French Revolution. Nevertheless, the declaration had a profound impact over popular ideas of human rights and inspired other writers and jurists. Napoleon's judicial reforms informed the 1866 four-volume Civil Code of Lower Canada, which remained in force in the province of Quebec until 1955.

The Declaration of the Rights of Man inspired other human rights documents over the course of the French Revolution. In 1791, French playwright Olympe de Gouges wrote *Déclaration des droits de la Femme et de la Citoyenne* (Declaration of the Rights of Woman and the Female Citizen) because the rights enshrined by the previous declaration had been extended to groups of men previously excluded from the political

process such as Protestants, Jews, and people of colour; women, however, remained outside the framework of the document. De Gouges dedicated her declaration to Louis XVI's consort, Queen Marie Antoinette, the most prominent woman in France's political culture at that time. Marie Antoinette was vilified in French revolutionary pamphlet literature for her Austrian origins and perceived immorality, but she had a long history of patronizing female writers and

A MAGNA CARTA FOR IMPERIAL RUSSIA?

In 1730, the death of Peter the Great's grandson, Peter II, caused a succession crisis in Imperial Russia. The Supreme Privy Council, consisting of representatives of the Russian nobility under the leadership of Prince Dmitry Mikhaylovich Golitsyn, gathered to discuss who would be Russia's next ruler from the available candidates, who included Peter the Great's surviving daughter and his three nieces. The council agreed to acclaim Peter's niece, Anna, a thirty-seven-year-old widow, as empress. Golitsyn and his allies assumed that Anna would be so grateful that she had been chosen over more senior members of her family that she would accept the authority of the Supreme Privy Council. Anna was offered the throne on the condition that she sign a charter that imposed limits on her power. This "Russian Magna Carta" declared that the empress needed permission from the council to marry, choose an heir, declare war or make peace, impose new taxes, or spend state revenues. Anna signed the charter, but publicly tore it up after she became empress and received a petition from members of the military and lesser gentry calling for her to rule as an autocrat. Anna never forgave the authors of the charter, and Prince Golitsyn died in prison during her reign, having been arrested for suspected involvement in a conspiracy against the empress. The failure of the Russian Magna Carta contributed to Russia remaining an autocratic monarchy until the twentieth century. A Russian ruler would not accept limits on his power until Nicholas II agreed to allow a form of representative government in 1905, just twelve years before the Russian Revolution of 1917.

The Fathers of Confederation met in London in 1866 to frame the British North America Act, setting up the Dominion of Canada in 1867.

artists, and de Gouges may have hoped that the queen would support universal rights for all women. Like Marie Antoinette, de Gouges was guillotined during the 1793–94 Reign of Terror.

Magna Carta had promised noblewomen freedom from forced marriages, and in 1442 all clauses of the charter were explicitly extended to English "ladies of great estate," but there had been few subsequent documents defending the rights of women until the eighteenth century. The Declaration of the Rights of Woman followed the precise structure of the Declaration of the Rights of Man, outlining rights for women according to the terms of the original document. De Gouges wrote:

The law should be the expression of the general will. All citizenesses and citizens should take part, in person or by their representatives, in its formation. It must be the same for everyone. All citizenesses and citizens, being equal in its eyes, should be equally admissible to all public dignities, offices and employments, according to their ability, and with no other distinction than that of their virtues and talents.

This call for equality of opportunity for all women was part of a larger trend of women's writing in the late eighteenth century, including *A Vindication of the Rights of Woman* by Mary Wollstonecraft. By the early twentieth century, advocates for women's suffrage were citing Magna Carta to demonstrate precedents for women's rights.

The Declaration of the Rights of Man and the other human rights charters drafted during the French Revolution demonstrate that by the eighteenth century the ideals of Magna Carta had spread beyond the English-speaking world. The authors of the declaration intended for its principles to spread beyond French borders, and this document inspired subsequent works that enshrined universal rights, including the United Nations' Universal Declaration of Human Rights.

MAGNA CARTA AND CANADA'S CONFEDERATION IN 1867

English Canada shares the political and legal inheritance of the rest of the English-speaking world, and Magna Carta influenced the terms of Canada's Confederation in 1867. The political and cultural environment of the nineteenth century meant that Magna Carta assumed a different legal and political significance in Canada than it did in the United States. The inhabitants of the thirteen colonies took specific clauses of Magna Carta literally according to the interpretations provided by Coke in the *Institutes of the Lawes of England* and the Petition of Right, particularly with regard to property law and individual rights. In contrast, Canadians came to view the Magna Carta as a foundation document for their system of parliamentary democracy and common law modelled on British political and legal institutions: the beginning of "the rule of law" tradition where everyone, even the monarch, became subject to the laws of the land.

By the time of Canada's Confederation in 1867, the differences between British and American interpretations of Magna Carta had become even more pronounced than it had been at the time of the American Revolution in the late eighteenth century. In the nineteenth-century United Kingdom (the official name for Great Britain and Ireland once their parliaments united in 1801), Parliament served as the guarantor of individual rights. The first Statute Laws Revision Act of 1856 began the process of removing "obsolete" legislation from the British statute books. Subsequent acts in 1861 and 1863 continued the process of removing centuries-old legislation from British statute books. The 1863 legislation repealed seventeen clauses from the 1225 version of Magna Carta issued by Henry III when he achieved his majority.

The British parliament's gradual removal of Magna Carta from the formal statute books attracted controversy. Members of Parliament argued that Magna

↖ Province House, Charlottetown, site of the Charlottetown Conference of 1864 that laid the groundwork for Confederation.

Carta and other "stones in the edifice of the constitution" should be exempt from statute reform.[13] Changes to forest law, guaranteed previously by Magna Carta and the Charter of the Forest, provoked opposition in the New Forest, which still maintained its own forest courts. Prominent cultural and political figures expressed concern that Magna Carta might be entering another period of obscurity as attempts to keep the individual clauses of the charter on British statute books were unsuccessful.

The private secondary schools and universities that trained the British Empire's future civil servants focused on classical learning rather than modern history and politics, a curriculum that was criticized by one of Canada's future governors general, John Campbell, Marquis of Lorne, who was educated at Eton, St. Andrews, and Cambridge. The poet Lord Byron satirized this emphasis on the classics in his 1806 verse, "Thoughts Suggested by a College Examination," writing, "Though marvelling at the name of Magna Carta / Yet well he recollects the laws of Sparta." Byron went on to complain in his poem that commentaries on Magna Carta gathered dust on the bookshelves of students while they studied classical Greece and Rome. Portrayals of Magna Carta in nineteenth-century popular culture focused on the perceived philosophy of the charter as a foundation document for British liberties rather than the individual clauses. This cultural climate would inform Magna Carta's significance for Canadians.

In contrast to the pace of developments in the United States because of the American Revolution, the process of self-government in Canada was a gradual one, undertaken in co-operation with the United Kingdom. The Province of Canada, consisting of parts of modern Ontario and Quebec, received a degree of autonomy in 1841, achieving Confederation with two of the Maritime Provinces in 1867. Canada did not receive control over its foreign policy until the Statute of Westminster created a separate Canadian crown in 1931. The Constitution was patriated in 1982, completing the process of sovereignty. The development of common law in English Canada followed the British model.

In 1867, the new Dominion of Canada became a constitutional monarchy with Queen Victoria as sovereign. Canada's first prime minister, John A. Macdonald, explained at the Quebec Conference of 1864, "The best interest and present and future prosperity of British North America will be promoted by a Federal union under the Crown of Great Britain, provided such union can be affected on principles just to the several provinces." The queen played an active role in Confederation, meeting in Britain with future prime minister John A. Macdonald and other Fathers of Confederation. The queen's support for Canada's self-government helped Macdonald bring together the four original provinces (Ontario, Quebec, New Brunswick, and Nova Scotia), which had very different economic and political interests at the time of Confederation.

Canada's system of government reflected the influence of Magna Carta, the Six Statutes, the Petition of Right, and the Bill of Rights, which had developed England's political system into the modern constitutional monarchy. The monarchy served as a unifying force for the new nation whose population included a sizable population of descendants of American loyalists who had immigrated to British North America at the time of the American Revolution. The Royal Proclamation and Quebec Act established the Crown as a guarantor of the

▶ Statue of Queen Victoria in front of Kensington Palace, London. The sculptor was Queen Victoria's daughter, Princess Louise, wife of the Marquis of Lorne, governor general of Canada from 1878 to 1883.

rights of minorities within the larger representative government, a perception of the monarchy that lasted in Quebec until the Quiet Revolution of the 1960s. John A. Macdonald's biographer, Richard Gwyn, observed that nineteenth-century Canadians celebrated their loyalty to the crown as a key cultural attribute that differentiated them from Americans.

> The potency of the ethic of loyalty, conjoining as it did an earthly sovereign with a heavenly one and a rule of law, was overwhelming. It made Canadians proud to be who they were (and not to be Americans) but ebulliently, braggartly proud. There was not the least shyness about Canada's loyalty. Flags were waved, songs were sung and public figures competed in their expressions of devotion to Crown and Queen.[14]

At the same time, royalty who visited Canada in the second half of the nineteenth century were warned not to expect undue deference because Canadians were a democratic people.

The Constitution Act, passed on July 1, 1867 (known as the British North America Act before 1982), established the modern division of powers between the federal government and the provinces that exists to the present day, combining the British parliamentary framework with a federal system of government. The act absorbed the legislative documents that shaped the development of the British government, including Magna Carta, the Petition of Right, the Bill of Rights, and the 1701 Act of Settlement, which governed succession to the throne until the 2013 succession reforms, as unwritten "conventions of the constitution." Within this framework, Canadians came to regard Magna Carta as the earliest legislative document that shapes modern Canadian politics and law. The Ontario provincial government's website states that its structure dates from Magna Carta. In 1941, future prime minister Lester B. Pearson declared that he was proud to be Canadian and part of a nation with a development that stretched from "Magna Carta to the Sirois Commission."[15] Magna Carta came to represent Canada's political and legal origins and would inform the Charter of Rights and Freedoms in the twentieth century.

◀ Canada's Parliament Buildings in the nineteenth century. Queen Victoria chose Ottawa as Canada's capital.

Part 5

Magna Carta Today

In the twenty-first century, Magna Carta informs politics and law on a global scale, including Canada. The year 2015 marked the eight-hundredth anniversary of John's reluctant acceptance of the terms imposed by his subjects in Magna Carta, but the charter remains a political, legal, and cultural touchstone. In 2005, the Right Honourable Lord Woolf declared, "eight hundred years on, Magna Carta's best days lie ahead. As an idea of freedom, democracy and the rule of law, it is lapping against the shores of tyranny." The influence of Magna Carta has spread beyond the Western world to influence independence movements in Africa and Asia and inform an international framework of human rights. The twenty-four surviving copies of Magna Carta from the thirteenth century, engrossed with the seals of John, Henry III, and Edward I, attract visitors to museums, cathedrals, and libraries in the United Kingdom, the United States, and Australia. Runnymede Meadow, where John affixed his seal to the original Magna Carta, has received visits from world leaders including the presidents of India and Hungary. In Canada, Magna Carta remains a formative influence on constitutional documents and judicial proceedings and is recognized as the foundation of the rights and freedoms enjoyed by Canadians.

THE GLOBAL IMPACT OF MAGNA CARTA AND THE CHARTER OF THE FOREST

For centuries, Magna Carta has enshrined equality before the law in the Western world, influencing the development of common law throughout the English-speaking world and the emergence of the constitutional monarchy in the United Kingdom and Commonwealth realms, including Canada. The charter was one of the key sources that informed the American Revolution and French Revolution. For the rest of the world, however, concepts of law and human rights derived from other sources, including religious and philosophical works and unwritten customs. The process of decolonization in the twentieth century inspired new generations of freedom fighters to invoke the charter to support independence movements around the world.

As nations came together to develop a common conception of human rights, the precedents set by

The United Nations General Assembly in New York.

Magna Carta informed the process. In 1941, American president Franklin Delano Roosevelt stated in his third inaugural address, "The democratic aspiration is no mere recent phase in human history. It is human history. It permeated the ancient life of early peoples. It blazed anew in the middle ages. It was written in Magna Charta." As nations achieved independence from former European empires over the course of the twentieth century, the new governments developed new constitutional documents and legislation that drew on a broad range of sources, including Magna Carta. The constitutions of newly independent nations were often described as national examples of Magna Carta. For example, the Objectives Resolution, which was adopted by Pakistan's legislative assembly in 1949, has become known as Pakistan's Magna Carta because it provided the fundamental principles for the governance of the nation, including democratic representation and Islam.[16] In India, its Supreme Court ruled that the right of every citizen to a passport arose from Magna Carta. The common law system informed by Magna Carta is in force in numerous Caribbean, African, and Pacific nations.

For freedom fighters around the world, Magna Carta served as an inspiration because of its role as the foundation of equality before the law. In his statement from the dock at the opening of the defence case in the Rivonia trial of 1964, future South African president Nelson Mandela declared his admiration for Magna Carta and the political institutions it shaped.

> The Magna Carta, the Petition of Rights, and the Bill of Rights are documents which are held in veneration by democrats throughout the world. I have great respect for British political institutions, and for the country's system of justice. . . . The American Congress, that country's doctrine of separation of powers, as well as the independence of its judiciary, arouses in me similar sentiments . . .[17]

When Mandela became president in 1994, after spending twenty-seven years in prison during the apartheid regime, one of his chief concerns was ensuring an independent judiciary for South Africa.

In international law, the U.N.'s Universal Declaration of Human Rights reflects the influence of Magna Carta

◤ Statue of Nelson Mandela in Johannesburg, South Africa.

and the subsequent documents it inspired, most notably the Declaration of the Rights of Man from the French Revolution. Canadian legal scholar John Peters Humphrey, who became the first director of the United Nations Division of Human Rights in 1946, authored the first draft of the declaration. Humphrey worked with the United Nations Commission of Human Rights, which included members from a broad range of political, religious, and cultural backgrounds.

Eleanor Roosevelt, a human rights activist and widow of President Frankin Roosevelt, chaired the U.N.'s nine-person drafting committee. Roosevelt recalled the lively debate over the creation of the document in her memoirs.

> The Declaration, [Vice-Chairman Peng Chung Chang of China] said, should reflect more than simply Western ideas and Dr. Humphrey would have to be eclectic in his approach . . . Dr. Humphrey joined enthusiastically in the discussion, and I remember that at one point Dr. Chang suggested that the Secretariat might well spend a few months studying the fundamentals of Confucianism![18]

The drafting of the declaration was an opportunity for Magna Carta to engage with legal and philosophical traditions around the world to create a framework of universal human rights.

On December 10, 1948, the Universal Declaration of Human Rights was adopted by the General Assembly with forty-eight countries, including Canada, voting in favour, none against, and eight abstentions. The text of the document reflected the strong influence of legal traditions that arose from Magna Carta and its successor documents. According to Article 6, "Everyone has the right to recognition everywhere as a person before the law." Article 7 states, "All are equal before the law and are entitled without any discrimination to equal protection of the law. All are entitled to equal protection against any discrimination in violation of this Declaration and against any incitement to such discrimination." Article 9 promises that "No one shall be subjected to arbitrary arrest, detention or exile." The precedents set by Magna Carta regarding freedom from forced marriage were also reflected in the charter, which declared, "Men and women of full age . . . are entitled to equal rights as to marriage, during marriage and at its dissolution" and "Marriage shall be entered into only with the free and full consent of the intending spouses."

Eleanor Roosevelt described the new document as "the international Magna Carta of all humankind,"[19] but there remained countries with reservations about this new human rights code. Saudi Arabia abstained from the vote on the grounds that equal marriage rights violated Islamic sharia law, an interpretation that was challenged and critiqued by representatives from Pakistan, a Muslim nation that voted in favour of the adoption of the declaration. South Africa also abstained from the vote, since the system of racial apartheid that existed there from 1948 to 1994 precluded equality before the law. The Soviet Union and other Eastern European countries in the Soviet bloc also abstained, objecting to the freedom of movement guaranteed by the declaration.

For the forty-eight countries that adopted the declaration, the terms served as non-binding ideals rather than international law. The development of the declaration into international law took decades as its clauses informed two binding United Nations human rights covenants: the International Covenant on Civil and Political Rights, and the International Covenant

MAGNA CARTA IN POPULAR CULTURE

Just as King John has entered popular culture as one of history's villains, Magna Carta has inspired literature, art, music, and film as the cornerstone of individual liberties. Rudyard Kipling's poem "What Say the Reeds at Runnymede?" (1911) celebrates the charter for its role in guaranteeing modern liberties, a perspective that reflects Edward Coke's seventeenth-century commentaries.

> At Runnymede, at Runnymede,
> Your rights were won at Runnymede!
> No freeman shall be fined or bound,
> Or dispossessed of freehold ground,
> Except by lawful judgment found
> And passed upon him by his peers.
> Forget not, after all these years,
> The Charter signed at Runnymede.

The poem was first published in *A School History of England* by C. R. L. Fletcher in 1911 and was intended to educate children about the influence of Magna Carta over modern society. Magna Carta has appeared on commemorative postage stamps around the world. A United Kingdom stamp from 1999 emphasized the key ideas codified in the charter, while an American stamp issued in 1965 to mark the 750th anniversary of Magna Carta emphasized the image of the king accepting terms from his subjects. The Ridley Scott film *Robin Hood* (2010) depicts John being pressured to sign a charter that would guarantee the rights of "all Englishmen." Magna Carta has also influenced music from Philip Sousa's Magna Carta March (1927) to Jay-Z's album *Magna Carta Holy Grail* (2013) as a symbol of liberty. The cover art for *Magna Carta Holy Grail* was displayed alongside one of the surviving copies of Magna Carta at Salisbury Cathedral in 2013, demonstrating the enduring impact of the charter on popular culture.

▼ This 1999 British postage stamp lists the human rights with precedents that date back to Magna Carta.

on Economic, Social, and Cultural Rights. Many other important international laws would follow, including the International Convention on the Elimination of All Forms of Racial Discrimination, the International Convention on the Elimination of Discrimination Against Women, and the United Nations Convention on the Rights of the Child. Over the course of his twenty-year career at the United Nations, Canadian John Humphrey oversaw the development and implementation of many of these human rights initiatives; in 1974, he received the Order of Canada "in recognition of his contributions to legal scholarship and his world-wide reputation in the field of human rights."[20] In 1993, 171 countries reiterated their commitment to human rights at the Vienna World Conference on Human Rights.

The 1217 Charter of the Forest, the piece of legislation in force for the longest time in English history, was finally superseded by the Wild Creatures and Forest Laws Act of 1971. The principle of common stewardship of shared resources assumed a new significance in the late twentieth century as indigenous peoples worldwide fought the environmental degradation of their traditional lands. In Bolivia, the principles codified in the Charter of the Forest inspired a 2009 Universal Declaration on the Rights of Mother Earth issued at a People's Summit with thirty-five thousand participants from 140 countries. Just as decolonization and the development of international law gave Magna Carta a new resonance after the Second World War, global environment movements brought the Charter of the Forest back into public consciousness, inspiring new debates on collective interest in shared resources.

SURVIVING COPIES OF MAGNA CARTA

The revival of interest in Magna Carta in the seventeenth century inspired a concerted effort to discover how many thirteenth-century editions of the charter survived. Today, there are twenty-four existing versions of Magna Carta dating from between 1215 and 1300, engrossed with the seal of John, Henry III, or Edward I. Seventeen versions of the charter predate 1300: four from 1215, one from 1216, four from 1217, four from 1225, and four from 1297. There are seven versions remaining from 1300. Today, Magna Carta is often invoked as though it is a single document; the existence of so many original engrossments seems surprising. The twenty-four documents that exist in modern times are, in fact, a small sample of the hundreds of official versions that circulated throughout the British Isles in the thirteenth century.

In John's reign, England consisted of thirty-nine counties formed between the fifth and eleventh centuries that would have all received copies of the Great charter for consultation in cathedrals, castles, and town halls. Since both the Welsh prince Llewelyn the Great and King Alexander III of Scotland supported the charter, versions of Magna Carta likely circulated in Wales and Scotland as well. A specially drafted Magna Carta Hiberniae was sent to Ireland in 1216 with "Dublin" substituted for "London" in the text. Original versions of the charter were intended to be accessible for consultation in legal disputes throughout the late Middle Ages and read aloud in county courts at regular intervals. For example, the bishop of Rochester brought a copy of Magna Carta to Parliament in 1404

The British Library houses two of the four surviving versions of Magna Carta from 1215.

and cited it in his arguments against what he considered to be illegal plans for new taxes on the clergy.

In these circumstances, there may once have been hundreds of official versions in the British Isles that eventually succumbed to neglect, fire, and periods of political and religious upheaval (such as the dissolution of the monasteries during the reign of Henry VIII and the English Civil Wars of the 1640s). Magna Carta Hibernae was destroyed in an explosion at Dublin's Four Courts in 1922, during the Irish Civil War. Surviving copies of Magna Carta have been discovered in numerous places, including cathedral libraries, country house attics, schools, and castle collections.

Of the four surviving engrossments of Magna Carta from 1215, two are in the British Library, one is in

Salisbury Cathedral, and one is in Lincoln Cathedral. For the eight-hundredth anniversary of Magna Carta, all four 1215 versions were displayed together at the British Library at the beginning of 2015. One of the British Library versions might well have been the first edition of Magna Carta reluctantly accepted by John in Runnymede Meadow. The document includes additions at the bottom of the main text, which may have been inserted at the last minute at the king's insistence before he would affix his seal.

After receiving the king's seal, this version of Magna Carta was stored at Dover Castle until it was presented to Sir Robert Cotton (1570–1631), an antiquarian and member of Parliament. When the Cotton Library at Ashburnham House, near London's Houses of Parliament, caught fire in 1731, Magna Carta was among the damaged documents. The yellow sealing wax melted, two holes were burned into the parchment, and the document shrivelled in the heat. The other 1215 edition of Magna Carta at the British Library also came from Cotton's collection but was undamaged in the fire. Its early history is unknown; legend has it, however, that Cotton rescued it from his tailor at the moment it was about to be cut into suit patterns.

The version of Magna Carta at Lincoln Cathedral is closely associated with Stephen Langton, who was educated at the Lincoln Cathedral School and may have provided this version for the cathedral library. The Lincoln Cathedral version of Magna Carta has been displayed at two World's Fairs: New York, in 1939, and Brisbane, Australia, in 1988. At the World's Fair in New York, Magna Carta was heavily guarded and displayed in a bulletproof case. As a symbol of liberty, there were fears Magna Carta would be a target for

Postage stamp commemorating the 1939 World's Fair in New York.

blockade of German U-boats, the United States agreed to store it in the vaults at Fort Knox, Kentucky. After the Japanese attack on Pearl Harbor in 1941, the U.S. Constitution and the Declaration of Independence were also moved from Washington for safekeeping to the secured facility of Fort Knox, Kentucky. Magna Carta returned to Lincoln Cathedral in 1946; a Thanksgiving service for the document's safe return, however, was disrupted by a woman in the congregation shouting, "I denounce Magna Carta: it is a relic and relics are denounced in the Bible." The Lincoln Cathedral Magna Carta returned to the United States for an eight-hundredth-anniversary touring exhibition in the autumn of 2014.

The version of Magna Carta at Salisbury Cathedral may have belonged to John's illegitimate half-brother, William Longspée, husband of Ela, Countess of Salisbury. Longspée was close to the king and influenced him to accept the demands of his barons. This copy of the charter was housed at Old Sarum Cathedral before being moved to the archives of the present Salisbury Cathedral, which also contains Longspée's effigy. The document went missing in the mid-seventeenth century during the course of repairs to the cathedral library but was rediscovered in the early nineteenth century.

The versions of Magna Carta outside the United Kingdom were discovered in unusual circumstances. The Ross Perot Family Foundation in the United States bought a 1297 version of the charter from the Brudenell family in 1984 for $1.5 million; it is currently on display at the National Archives in Washington, D.C. The Brudenells, relatives of the nineteenth-century earls of Cardigan, realized they had the document in their

terrorists. These fears were justified. A homemade bomb exploded near the British pavilion on July 4, 1940, killing two New York City police officers.

The outbreak of the Second World War extended the document's time in the United States. Rather than risk returning the document to England through a

◀ Salisbury Cathedral houses a 1215 version of Magna Carta that may have belonged to King John's half-brother.

possession in 1974 following an inventory of the family records. After this discovery, their Magna Carta spent several years resting on an easel in a room at Deene Park, the family estate, before the sale. In 2007, the "American" Magna Carta went up for auction at Sotheby's and was sold to American businessman David Rubenstein for $21.3 million and remains on public display.

The "Australian" Magna Carta, a 1297 version on display in Parliament House, emerged from the King's School library in Bruton, Somerset. This document was originally sent to the sheriff of Surrey, Robert de Glamorgan, to be proclaimed in the county court, and it spent an unspecified amount of time in a Sussex nunnery before being acquired by the King's School before the 1930s. The Australian government bought the document in 1952 for public exhibition, demonstrating the centrality of the charter to politics and the law throughout the English-speaking world.

The other engrossments of Magna Carta from the reigns of Henry III

A stamp commemorating the Canadian Charter of Rights and Freedoms.

and Edward I are scattered throughout collections in the United Kingdom. One-quarter of these documents are housed in the Bodleian Library at Oxford University. A 1217 Magna Carta from Oxford spent time in Canada in 2010 after a New York exhibition. The eruption of Iceland's Mount Eyjafjallajökull temporarily grounded flights to the United Kingdom, stranding the document in the United States. The travel delays provided time for the Manitoba Legislature to negotiate a loan of Magna Carta for a three-month exhibition there.

MAGNA CARTA IN MODERN CANADA

Magna Carta informs the Canadian Bill of Rights and the Charter of Rights and Freedoms and continues to be cited in Canadian legal proceedings. While there is a broad consensus that Magna Carta informs common law in English Canada and the parliamentary system of government, the question of whether the terms of Magna Carta are binding legislation in Canada has been debated in courtrooms from the early twentieth century to the present day. A series of judicial rulings made clear that the actual text of Magna Carta is not binding despite the historical significance of the document.

Magna Carta has been cited in court cases, demonstrating its formative impact on the legal system in English Canada. For example, in the decision of Blencoe v. British Columbia (Human Rights Commission), which came before the Supreme Court of Canada in 2000, Justice Louis LeBel stated: "The notion that justice delayed is justice denied reaches back to the mists of time. In Magna Carta in 1215, King John promised: 'To none will we sell, to none will we deny, or delay, right or justice.'" This argument presents a clear link between King John accepting Magna Carta in 1215 and modern Canadian law.

The Ontario Provincial Legislature, Queen's Park, Toronto.

While the ideas within Magna Carta continue to shape the Canadian legal system, the actual text of the charter is not formally part of the current constitution and is subject to provincial or federal legislation. Canadian constitutional scholar Peter Hogg wrote that Magna Carta was an English statute amenable to ordinary legislation.[21] The question of whether the charter is legally binding in Canada has been a frequent point of contention in twentieth- and twenty-first-century cases in British Columbia. In 1978 the R. v. Dobell case struck down the theory "that if there were a disparity between a term in the Magna Carta and the Criminal Code of Canada the Magna Carta should override the Criminal Code of Canada."[22] The British Columbia Court of Appeal ruled in 2003: "Unlike the Canadian Charter of Rights and Freedoms, the Magna Carta is not a constitutional document."[23] These legal cases demonstrate a key difference between perceptions of Magna Carta in Canada and the United States, where the charter is treated as a totemic document that is literally part of the fabric of American law.

Magna Carta informed the development of Canada's Bill of Rights, a federal statute from 1960 that was the earliest written expression of human rights law at the federal level in Canada. The Bill of Rights replaced the unwritten rights implied by the 1867 Constitution Act that the new nation would be created "with a Constitution similar in Principle to that of the United Kingdom," a statement that indicates Magna Carta, the Petition of Right, and the Bill of Rights are all part of the Canadian constitutional tradition. The Bill of Rights made a number of the unwritten provisions in Canada's constitutional tradition explicit, including rights that date back to Magna Carta and its successor documents, including "the right of the individual to life, liberty, security of the person and enjoyment of property, and the right not to be deprived thereof except by due process of law" and "the right of the individual to equality before the law and the protection of the law." Despite its historical precedents, the Bill of Rights was not universally applicable because it was a federal statute that has not been ratified by the provinces. The creation of the Charter of Rights and Freedoms in 1982 addressed the shortcomings of the Bill of Rights, giving the rights that date from Magna Carta constitutional status.

The text of the Charter of Rights and Freedoms (1982) reflects the influence of Magna Carta and the Canadian Bill of Rights. Section 9 of the charter guarantees freedom from arbitrary detainment or imprisonment, reflecting the lasting influence of clause 39 of the 1215 Magna Carta. Section 10 guarantees habeas corpus, a summons with the force of a court order, it proves lawful authority to detain a prisoner, a right that dates back to the Five Knights case that precipitated the Petition of Right in 1628. The Charter also affirms the primacy of the Royal Proclamation of 1763 as Canada's first constitutional document, stating that the charter does not abrogate from any of the rights or freedoms recognized by the proclamation.

In addition to Magna Carta, the Charter of the Forest has also had a formative impact on attitudes toward the environment and crown land in Canada. The charter set precedents regarding public access to crown land and the idea that this land is held in trust for the benefit of all Canadians. For example, the British Columbia Commission on Resources and Environment, established in 1992, produced the Land Use Charter, which encouraged community consensus in the development of crown land.

Eight hundred years after its creation, the ideals codified in Magna Carta have spread around the world, shaping politics and law in a global context. In Canada, Magna Carta has a unique history, influencing the relationship between the Crown and First Nations from the Royal Proclamation of 1763, Canada's Confederation in 1867, and the modern Bill of Rights and the Charter of Rights and Freedoms. Magna Carta shaped the development of common law in English Canada and continues to be cited in judicial proceedings. Canada's constitutional monarchy reflects the precedents set by Magna Carta, the Petition of Right, and the British Bill of Rights. For eight hundred years, Magna Carta has given its gifts to Canada and the world and will continue to do so for centuries to come.

Acknowledgements

Just as Magna Carta received the support of twenty-five barons in 1215, the writing of this book would not have been possible without the assistance of many people.

First and foremost, I would like to thank the Magna Carta Canada co-chairs, Suzy and Len Rodness, for bringing the Magna Carta to Canada in 2015 and inviting me to write this book. Suzy first asked me to contribute articles to the Magna Carta Canada website in the autumn of 2013 after attending one of my lectures at the University of Toronto, School of Continuing Studies, and I have had the pleasure of working with Magna Carta Canada ever since. Suzy and Len have provided invaluable support throughout this project, including connecting me with Dundurn Press, and assistance with sourcing illustrations and publicity. Without them, this book would not have been written.

I would like to acknowledge Durham Cathedral for the loan of a Magna Carta from the reign of King Edward I for the Magna Carta Canada touring exhibition, Gordon Summerbell and Bernadette Toner for planting the seed which led to the loan, and the four Canadian venues hosting the exhibition: the Canadian Museum of History, Fort York National Historic Site, the Canadian Museum for Human Rights, and the Legislative Assembly of Alberta Visitor Centre.

A special thanks to the Honourable Andrew Scheer, Speaker of the House of Commons, for contributing the foreword.

At Dundurn Press, I would like to thank my editor, Michael Melgaard, for his helpful feedback on the manuscript, and my publicist, Karen McMullin. I would also like to thank Kirk Howard, Margaret Bryant, Sheila Douglas, Carrie Gleason, Jonathan Schmidt, and the rest of the team at Dundurn.

I would like to thank the Ontario Arts Council Writers' Reserve Program for its generous financial support of this project.

I would like to thank Trajectory for designing the Plantagenet family tree, and Jonathan Lee for taking the author photo.

Thanks also go to the members of the Magna Carta Canada Education Committee, Steve Tsimikalis, Paul Sischy, Matt Mooney, Bronwyn Graves, and Nathan Tidridge; and the co-presidents and vice-president of Lord Cultural Resources, Gail and Barry Lord, and Maria Piacente.

I have had Magna Carta on my mind for many months. I would like to thank my grandparents, Bob Hanbidge and Mary Harris, and my brother, David Harris, for listening to me talk, at length, about King John and his barons. I would also like to thank Leigh-Ann Coffey for her advice on this project.

In 2001, I visited England for the first time with my parents, Richard and Sue Harris, and brother. We visited numerous historic sites, including Runnymede Meadow, contributing to a lifelong love of history. I would like to thank my parents for encouraging my love of history and being there for me every step of the way.

Since I completed my Ph.D. in 2012, my career as a historian has gone in many interesting directions. My husband, Bruce Harpham, has been loving and supportive through all these changes. Marrying Bruce remains the best decision I have ever made.

Appendix 1
The Magna Carta 2015 Exhibition

"All of this innocently began as one of many items on our list of 'empty nester' activities, yet it quickly elbowed aside all other considerations and succeeded in capturing our combined imaginations and energies for the better part of the last four years of our lives." So wrote Len and Suzy Rodness of Toronto in 2014, describing the genesis of the idea of bringing Magna Carta to Canada four years earlier. They began by consulting a friend at their son's school.

"A friendship with Bernadette Toner, a gracious, transplanted English bursar at our son's school afforded us the opportunity to spearhead a venture to bring the priceless piece of parchment that is Magna Carta to Canada in celebration of its eight-hundredth birthday."

To their delight, this dedicated couple were able to gain the agreement of Durham Cathedral, home of several Magna Carta documents, to lend two of these treasures for exhibition on a limited tour of Canada on the eight-hundredth anniversary in 2015, if sufficient museum-quality venues could be found to display, protect, and preserve them, and if the necessary funding could be raised. The exhibition would not only benefit Canadians but would contribute toward the cost of the continuing conservation of these precious historic documents.

So Magna Carta Canada was founded as a not-for-profit charitable organization dedicated to meeting these conditions and making the tour possible. Len and Suzy served as its co-chairs and began encouraging others to join them and to contribute to their fundraising campaign, an experience that taught them a lot about Magna Carta and about Canada.

"Our figurative journey back in time to an English meadow on a summer's day in 1215 has served to not only enhance our knowledge of the parry and thrust of mediaeval politics and society but it has sharpened our awareness of the gift that is our country today. Each and every boardroom pitch and cocktail party conversation that were met with the remark 'I remember something about Magna Carta from school but what it is exactly, I cannot say' propelled us to lean harder into our endeavour."

With fundraising underway, Magna Carta Canada engaged Lord Cultural Resources, the Canadian firm that is a world leader in museum exhibition planning, first to secure potential venues for Magna Carta and then to plan and design the exhibition. As Len and Suzy explained their objective to Co-Presidents Gail and Barry Lord and the company's Vice-President for Exhibitions Maria Piacente, "Bringing Magna Carta to our shores to us meant providing all Canadians with a tactile, tangible, teachable moment. What an extraordinary opportunity to be able to stand squarely before the document that is arguably the quickening moment of our fully developed democratic ideals, rule of law, and human rights standards."

Drawing on their experience in planning, designing, or assisting museum-quality venues across Canada, Lord Cultural Resources was able to find four venues that were eager to display Magna Carta (see appendix 2).

While this outstanding series of venues for Magna Carta was being lined up, Len and Suzy Rodness and their steering committee continued their campaign to raise the funds to make their dream a reality. Although many generous donors contributed, the breakthrough moment came in 2014 when Magna Carta Canada was successful in obtaining federal government funding for the tour. Len and Suzy were able to proclaim, "2015 will be Canada's moment to fix our collective national gaze on this transformative instrument whose notes echo through the centuries and continue to serenade us to this day."

Lord Cultural Resources could then continue with the detailed design and tendering of construction of the exhibition, placed in a setting suggesting Runnymede, the meadow where on June 15, 1215, a group of British barons forced King John of England to affix his seal to the original version of Magna Carta. The exhibition featured figures of the barons, commoners, and King John, along with banners, panels, and touch screens that related the roles of each in the struggle against the king's imperious demands for everyone to sacrifice their lives and their resources for his interminable (and unsuccessful) wars with France. Throughout the exhibition, written and spoken quotations about Magna Carta reminded visitors that the principles advanced in these Great Charters have been a subject for many fine minds for centuries. The displays included the following six outstanding clusters of exhibits.

THE PRECIOUS DOCUMENTS

In 1300, John's grandson, Edward I, voluntarily reissued Magna Carta to show that it would apply to every ruler of England thereafter. The two main display cases in the exhibition featured the two precious documents on loan from Durham Cathedral — one of Edward's authorized 1300 versions and the 1300 Charter of the Forest. The 1300 Great Charter was shown in a tent symbolizing the one in which King John would have received the barons, while the Charter of the Forest was nestled in a forest-like setting. In order to ensure preservation of these precious documents, they had to be exhibited in climate-controlled cases with subdued light.

THE "DIGITAL CHARTER"

The charters are written in medieval Latin, the legal and clerical language of the day, but the exhibition used twenty-first-century technology to enable visitors to read them both in English, exploring key themes that explained why these documents were and remain so important. Habeas corpus, for example, the require-ment that the Crown cannot incarcerate anyone unless it can produce evidence of his or her wrongdoing, trial by jury, and the right of a widow not to be forced to remarry, thereby giving up her property, are just a few of the rights and protections that began with Magna Carta. Key words throughout the exhibit — Rights,

Privileges, Liberties, Justice, and Law among them — reminded visitors of some of the fundamental concepts that originated in Magna Carta.

A GLOBAL LEGACY

A large three-dimensional globe in the exhibition helped visitors to appreciate the impact of these historic documents all around the world over the past eight hundred years. In the United States, of course, the Declaration of Independence, the Constitution, and the Bill of Rights are all direct descendants of Magna Carta. In France, the 1789 Declaration of the Rights of Man that sparked the French Revolution is the best-known example, but the French Charter of 1814 that limited the rights of King Louis XVIII when he was restored to the throne after the fall of Napoleon was equally important as the basis of the rule of law and due process that continues in France to this day. On the other side of the globe, the Indian Constitution of 1947 includes a vital section on all Indian citizens' fundamental rights of equality before the law that follows the model of Magna Carta. Australia and New Zealand are among other former British colonies similarly affected. And, of course, the United Nations' Universal Declaration of Human Rights in 1948 gave us what many see as the most important long-term legacy of Magna Carta, extending the concept of human rights to everyone regardless of their citizenship, ethnic origin, or country of residence. We are still struggling to live up to its intention, which was to ensure that atrocities like the Holocaust would never happen again.

THE GREAT CHARTERS AND CANADA

"Responsible government" — a concept that was first advanced in Magna Carta — was the goal of both William Lyon Mackenzie and Louis-Joseph Papineau in the rebellions they led against the British colonial administration in 1837–39. Canadians enjoy responsible government and the rule of law today, based on principles that were first advanced — albeit in limited form — in these Great Charters. Many sections of the act that created the Confederation of Canada in 1867 manifest the legacy of the charter. Even more so our 1982 Charter of Rights and Freedoms is directly modelled on it. The connections of these and other documents with Magna Carta were shown in an exhibit that linked the heritage of Magna Carta to Canada, including the controversies and struggles in our history to preserve the spirit of the documents. Canada's First Nations, for example, maintained a culture of stewardship of their lands comparable to the vision of the Charter of the Forest, but colonial settlement seldom respected it. A large-scale reproduction of the Royal Proclamation of 1763, which has been called "the indigenous people's Magna Carta," showed that it was indeed the first recognition by the British Crown that Canada's Native population had rights. The proclamation has been invoked in land claims disputes ever since.

THE RIGHTS OF "FREE MEN" (ONLY?)

Although it affirmed the right of widows to refuse to be ordered to remarry and thereby forfeit their property, Magna Carta did not otherwise recognize women as persons, since they were considered to belong to their fathers or husbands. Three or four centuries later when the slave trade made some men rich, no one extended rights to this human merchandise. Colonized peoples were similarly not recognized as people with equal rights. In the exhibition, excerpts from historical documents described these limitations of the original concepts and the ongoing struggle to extend these rights to all, in England and around the world, over the past eight centuries.

THE MEDIA WALL OF JUSTICE TODAY

More twenty-first-century technology lit up the final section of the exhibition with a touch-screen Media Wall that encouraged visitors to explore contemporary struggles for justice and human rights. Visitors were asked to vote for the most important clauses in Magna Carta, to draft a contemporary charter, and to design a seal for it.

The Magna Carta Canada 2015 exhibition tour enabled Canadians to appreciate all the more keenly how important the principles of these documents are, and how important it is for us all to protect them.

Appendix 2

The Venues

CANADIAN MUSEUM OF HISTORY

Gatineau, Quebec

Located on the shores of the Ottawa River in Gatineau, Quebec, the Canadian Museum of History is one of Canada's largest and most popular cultural institutions, attracting over one million visitors each year. The museum's principal role is to enhance Canadians' knowledge, understanding, and appreciation of the events, experiences, people, and objects that have shaped Canada's history and identity, as well as to foster appreciation of world history and culture. The museum safeguards a collection of over three million artifacts and specimens, including some of Canada's most valued national treasures. It is home to the Canadian Children's Museum and an IMAX® Theatre. The Canadian Museum of History is a federal Crown corporation that is also responsible for the Canadian War Museum.

FORT YORK NATIONAL HISTORIC SITE

Toronto, Ontario

Built in 1793 to protect the newly founded Town of York, Fort York National Historic Site is the birthplace of urban Toronto. It is best known as the location where the Battle of York came to its violent climax in April 1813 during the War of 1812. The fort served as the city's primary harbour defence between the 1790s and the 1880s. It was the home of a military garrison until the early 1930s when the site was transformed into a municipal museum.

Today, the fort's defensive walls enclose Canada's largest collection of original War of 1812 buildings. A visitor centre opened in 2014 outside the walls to provide orientation to the full forty-three-acre National Historic Site and to supply exhibition spaces capable of displaying extraordinary objects like Magna Carta.

John Graves Simcoe, the first lieutenant governor of

Upper Canada, established Fort York. The links between Simcoe and the fort make it a fitting place to explore Magna Carta's legacy. Simcoe not only set up the province's democratic institutions but championed a law passed in 1793 to prevent the further introduction of slaves into Upper Canada and allow for the gradual abolition of slavery — an act without precedent in the British Empire.

CANADIAN MUSEUM FOR HUMAN RIGHTS

Winnipeg, Manitoba

As Canada's national museum mandated to enhance understanding of human rights, promote respect, and encourage reflection and dialogue, the Canadian Museum for Human Rights (CMHR) is a fitting host venue for the Magna Carta Canada 2015 Tour.

Opened in September 2014, the CMHR is the only museum in the world devoted to human rights awareness and education.

Using the latest technologies, the oldest forms of storytelling, and the timeless power of art, hundreds of stories are woven into a rich tapestry that relays the importance of human rights for all.

Every visitor experience is a combination of amazing interactions with architecture and content. The building itself is a stunning new international architectural icon; complex geometry and human rights symbolism grace every component.

The museum's galleries are built around human rights themes; the relevance and links between its content, Magna Carta, and the Charter of the Forest are plentiful. The fact that Her Majesty Queen Elizabeth II, queen of Canada, presented the museum with a stone from Runnymede (birthplace of the Magna Carta) makes it even more appropriate a place to see the exhibition.

The CMHR is the first national museum built outside of Ottawa and is located in Winnipeg, Manitoba, for good reason. The city has an inspiring human rights legacy.

LEGISLATIVE ASSEMBLY OF ALBERTA VISITOR CENTRE

Edmonton, Alberta

An iconic part of Alberta's history, the Alberta Legislature is an architectural rarity and marvel. Officially opened in 1912, the legislature is where the eighty-seven members of the Legislative Assembly meet to debate and discuss public policy. The building is open to visitors 362 days a year, and free guided tours are offered daily. Departing regularly through the day, these tours cover a number of topics, including the

formation of the province, the history of the Alberta Legislative Assembly, parliamentary traditions, and our democratic roots. The tour is not only about government and politics; however, guides explore the building's unique and stunning architectural heritage as well as the numerous works of art on display inside. On any given day, the legislature is a hub of activity, with people coming to enjoy the grounds' natural beauty and seasonal activities, including wading pools and a skating rink. An on-site retail shop, Alberta Made, features art and fine crafts made by Alberta artists, while the adjacent Interpretive Centre displays a number of Alberta-themed exhibits. Both are great places to explore.

Our parliamentary traditions are based on fundamental principles established by the Magna Carta, and the Alberta Legislature is the perfect venue to showcase the document. The Great Charter has a direct impact on the rights and freedoms Albertans experience today, and we are honoured to showcase this exhibit for Albertans to come and visit.

Appendix 3

The Durham Cathedral Magna Carta

Durham Cathedral has been a place of worship, welcome, and hospitality for almost a millennium. Built in 1093 to house the Shrine of St. Cuthbert, the cathedral is cherished for its magnificent Romanesque architecture and incomparable setting at the heart of a UNESCO World Heritage Site. It is famous as the Shrine of St. Cuthbert and the resting place of the Venerable Bede.

Originally built as a monastic cathedral for a community of Benedictine monks, Durham Cathedral possesses some of the most intact surviving monastic buildings in England, including the medieval cloister, the Monks' Dormitory, and the Western Undercroft. The nave, quire, and transepts are all Norman, and the nave boasts what is believed to be the world's first structural pointed arch.

With its dramatic position at the top of the Durham City peninsula, Durham Cathedral is both physically and symbolically a focal point for the community of Durham and the wider northeast region. It is also one of Britain's best-loved buildings.

The architectural and historical importance of Durham Cathedral was recognized in 1986 when the Durham World Heritage Site was inscribed as one of the first UNESCO World Heritage Sites in the United Kingdom.

Durham Cathedral holds three copies of Magna Carta, as well as three copies of the Forest Charter, composed in 1217 to protect the rights of those who dwelt within the royal forest.

The exemplifications of Magna Carta at Durham comprise the issue of November 1216, the issue of February 11, 1225, and the issue of March 28, 1300.

The earliest of the Durham Cathedral copies of Magna Carta, the November 1216 Bristol exemplar, is the only known copy of this issue to survive. It contains forty-two clauses (as compared to the sixty-one of the 1215 issue).

The 1225 issue of the Magna Carta held at Durham Cathedral is one of four surviving exemplars. Issued when Henry III reached the age of majority, it is a shorter version (thirty-seven articles), a concession of liberties in return for a fifteenth part of movable goods. It includes the new statement that the charter was issued spontaneously and of the king's own free will. This was the first version of the charter to enter English law. The Durham copy is in a neat chancery-style hand. The accompanying 1225 Forest Charter at Durham is one of three surviving copies.

The final Magna Carta at Durham is the issue of March 28, 1300 (DUL DCD 2.2.Reg.2), the last full exemplification. Except for a marginal hole not affecting the text, the copy is in excellent condition — the best, in fact, of the six surviving copies.

The provenance of the exemplifications of Magna Carta at Durham is difficult to trace. However, three of the surviving 1215 originals come from cathedrals, suggesting that bishops were responsible for the distribution and custody of the charter. This reflects the fact that sheriffs were the object of inquiry under the charter and could not therefore, as would normally have been the case, be entrusted with the charter's publication.

All three copies of Magna Carta will be displayed in Durham Cathedral itself when new exhibition spaces open in 2017 as part of the cathedral's redevelopment project Open Treasure.

Notes

1. Peter Coss, "An Age of Deference," in *A Social History of England 1200–1500*, ed. Rosemary Horrox and W. Mark Ormrod (Cambridge: Cambridge University Press, 2006), 31.
2. Christopher Gravett, *English Medieval Knight 1200–1300* (New York: Osprey Publishing, 2002), 9.
3. Kathryn Faulkner, "The Transformation of Knighthood in Early Thirteenth-Century England," in *The English Historical Review* 111:440 (February 1996): 1–23.
4. Richard Britnell, "Town Life," in *A Social History of England 1200–1500,* eds. by Rosemary Horrox and W. Mark Ormrod (Cambridge: Cambridge University Press, 2006), 145.
5. See Graham E. Seel, *King John: An Underrated King* (London: Anthem Press, 2012).
6. Giraldus Cambrensis, *Expurgnatio Hibernica: The Conquest of Ireland* (Dublin: F.X. Martin, 1978), 237–39.
7. Seel, *King John*, 48.

8. Richard Brooks, *The Knight Who Saved England: William Marshall and the French Invasion, 1217* (Oxford: Osprey Publishing, 2014), 165.

9. Clayton Roberts and David Roberts, A *History of England, Prehistory to 1714* (Upper Saddle River, NJ: Prentice Hall, 1991), 123.

10. Sir Edward Coke, *Debates in Commons*, cited in A.E. Dick Howard, *Magna Carta Text and Commentary*, rev. ed. (Charlottesville: University Press of Virginia, 1998), 4.

11. Leslie MacKinnon, "Royal Proclamation of 1763, Canada's 'Indian Magna Carta' Turns 250," CBC News, October 6, 2013, www.cbc.ca/news/politics/royal-proclamation-of-1763-canada-s-indian-magna-carta-turns-250-1.1927667.

12. Anonymous, *L'Angleterre Instruisant la France ou Tableau: Historique et Politique du Regne de Charles I et de Charles II: Servant d'introduction a la Relation de la mort cr . . . et b . . . de Charles I, suivie de sa harangue sur l'echaffaud. Discite justitiam moniti, et non temnere divos* (London and Paris: Chez Lepetit, 1793).

13. Ralph V. Turner, "The Meaning of Magna Carta Since 1215," *History Today* 53, no. 9 (2003), www.historytoday.com/ralph-v-turner/meaning-magna-carta-1215.

14. Richard Gwyn, *John A.: The Man Who Made Us*, vol. 1 (Toronto: Vintage Canada, 2008), 366.

15. Andrew Cohen, *Lester B. Pearson* (Toronto: Penguin Group, 2008), 73.

16. James Wynbrandt, *A Brief History of Pakistan* (New York: Facts on File, 2009), 171.

17. Nelson Mandela, "Statement from the Dock at the Opening of the Defence Case in the Rivonia Trial, Pretoria Supreme Court," African National Congress, April 20, 1964, www.anc.org.za/show.php?id=3430.

18. Eleanor Roosevelt, *The Autobiography of Eleanor Roosevelt* (New York: Harper and Brothers, 1961), 317.

19. Canadian Council on International Law, "John P. Humphrey 1905–1995," www.ccil-ccdi.ca/ccil-about-humphrey/2011/1/29/john-p-humphrey-1905-1995.html

20. Canadian Council on International Law, "John P. Humphrey 1905–1995," www.ccil-ccdi.ca/ccil-about-humphrey/2011/1/29/john-p-humphrey-1905-1995.html.

21. See R.V. Jebbett, 2003, BCCA, 69.

22. Andrew Kitching, "The Magna Carta and Canada's Constitution." (Ottawa: Library of Parliament, 2005), 4.

23. Ibid., 2.

For Further Reading

Carpenter, David. *Magna Carta.* New York: Penguin Classic, 2015.

Danzinger, Danny, and John Gillingham. *1215: The Year of Magna Carta*, New York: Simon & Schuster, 2005.

Hogg, Peter. *Constitutional Law of Canada, 2010.* Toronto: Carswell, 2010.

Hogue, Arthur R. *Origins of the Common Law.* Indianapolis, IN: Liberty Fund Inc., 2010.

Holland, Randy J. *Magna Carta: Muse and Mentor.* New York: Thomson Reuters, 2014.

Holt, J.C. *Magna Carta*. Cambridge: Cambridge University Press, 2015.

Horrox, Rosemary, and W. Mark Ormrod. *A Social History of England, 1200–1500.* Cambridge: Cambridge University Press, 2006.

Hunt, Lynn. *The French Revolution and Human Rights: A Brief Documentary History.* Boston: Bedford/St. Martin's, 1996.

Jackson, Michael, and Philippe Lagassé. *Canada and the Crown: Essays on Constitutional Monarchy*. Kingston and Montreal, McGill-Queen's University Press, 2013.

Loengard, Janet S. *Magna Carta and the England of King John*. Woodbridge: Boydell Press, 2010.

Tidridge, Nathan. *Canada's Constitutional Monarchy: An Introduction to Our Form of Government*. Toronto: Dundurn, 2011.

Turner, Ralph V. *King John: England's Evil King?* United Kingdom: The History Press, 2005.

——————. *Magna Carta: Through the Ages*. Harlow: Pearson, 2003.

Vincent, Nicholas. *Magna Carta: A Very Short Introduction*. Oxford: Oxford University Press, 2012.

——————. *Magna Carta: The Foundation of Freedom, 1215–2015*: London: Third Millennium Publishing, 2015.

Illustration Credits